A SPIRITUAL GUIDE
—— FOR ——
RETIREMENT

GEORGE M. BROCKWAY, PH.D.

authorHOUSE®

AuthorHouse™
1663 Liberty Drive
Bloomington, IN 47403
www.authorhouse.com
Phone: 1 (800) 839-8640

Published by AuthorHouse 06/23/2016

ISBN: 978-1-5246-1355-6 (sc)
ISBN: 978-1-5246-1354-9 (e)

Library of Congress Control Number: 2016909471

Print information available on the last page.

Front Cover Photo taken by Karin E. Ringheim

CONTENTS

Two basic meanings of 'spiritual':

   the *humanistic* meaning, that which honors, nurtures
   and enjoys the distinctly human parts of us
and
   the *religious* meaning, that which holds there is
   some transcendent reality, some non-physical reality,
   whether a soul or a God or an afterlife, or all three.

The assumptions behind naturalism, both metaphysical
and epistemological.

Using Buddhism as the referent (often, but not exclusively). The assumptions behind the religious spiritual, both metaphysical and epistemological.

Isn't the issue rather: are you happy? And how do you live and interact with others?
If either position on the 'spiritual' leads to the same actions or behaviors, does it make any difference which *worldview* one adopts?

And what is "happiness"?
That depends on what you think is valuable and good, what is worth having and worth seeking. In both

the non-moral realm . . . and

How the religious spiritualist gets *there* (to how one *ought* to live).

> Metaphysical grounds: all equally created by God and endowed . . .

> Textual and obedience grounds: "Love one another as . . ."

How the secular humanist gets *there* (to how one *ought* to live).

> Contractual and rational grounds. (Rawls & Dworkin)

But *is* this "there" the same?

At the initial level . . . . and at a subsequent level.

There are two such.
But are these just wishful thinking on the part of the religious spiritual?

Each (the O/S H and the RS) holds a worldview, a theory or **an explanatory framework,** for understanding and comprehending what is the case, – for what is true about our lives and for *how they fit or don't into the universe.*

And each explanatory framework has assumptions or axioms (now five such), which it takes as fundamental and given, not able or needing to be defended or proven. Which set do you find the most . . . . . . helpful? Any need to choose?

Through that "more fully human life."

If reason and logic can't settle the issue, then what?

INTRODUCTION

Retirement. What a great . . . and an unusual time. A time in our lives which most of the world's population never reaches. (Think of that.) What a gift! And what I mean by retirement here is simply: being in a position where you no longer *have to* work in order to survive. You may choose to continue working, but not because you have to but because you want to, because that's how you enjoy spending some or all of your time.

Consider how much of our lives we do *have to* work if we're going to survive, i.e. have enough food, shelter, clothing, health care and formal education to lead a minimally decent human life, and certainly to have any chance of leading a more fully human life. We have to work for it. At least, the swamping majority of human beings on the planet must do so. But there may come a time, if you've been disciplined and lucky, when you no longer need to work to ensure your survival. A condition not that many, worldwide, ever enjoy. And the further back in history we go, the less that number becomes. A gift indeed.

So what are you going to do with this gift? Finally take some time to "smell the roses"? Sounds good, but is it enough? I'm going to argue that it's not enough or, more accurately, that "smelling the roses" fully understood actually encompasses much more than simply kicking back on some Caribbean beach with an umbrella drink and watching the sun cross the sky.

It can be a time to take the measure of your life so far. What have you done? What do you still want to do? Where are you going in and with the rest of your life? What do you want it to represent?

In the Hindu culture, e.g., one's life is thought of as divided into various stages. There is the student stage where your 'job' is to play, then go to school and learn what you need to know in order to take your place in and contribute to the greater society and your family. Then there is the stage of the householder where you're now having your family, raising your children, working at your job and taking part in civil life. Working at having an effect on the larger society around you and in which you live and move and have your being. But eventually (and hopefully), you get beyond those needs and responsibilities (or someone else is carrying them for you!). Then you can enter into what is called the stage of the "forest dweller". Here, the theory is, you can leave behind all those tasks and responsibilities that occupied you during the householder stage and go off into the forest to meditate on what it's all meant and whether or not the claims of the Hindu religion which you grew up with are really true. Is it the case, e.g., that you already are, at your deepest core, just one with Brahman (*Tat Tvam Asi*) and that your basic purpose is to come to realize that oneness? Is that what life really is and is all about? Finally, and assuming you come to the conclusion that that is true, you return to society in the fourth stage, that of the *sannyasin,* one who neither loves nor hates anything, one who can be in the world without being overcome or swayed by its blandishments and temptations, one who can continue to nurture within him or herself that vision of oneness with Brahman.

These last two stages don't translate very easily or well into our culture. (And not least because traditionally they were meant only for men.) But in one respect we may be able to take a page from their playbook. The respect in which we too, when we enter into retirement, typically have more time on our hands to spend on whatever we want to spend it on. And, we're presuming here, the means to do so. In that vein, this book is for those who would like to spend at least some of that extra time looking into "what it's all about?"

And thus, admittedly, this book is intended mainly for a western audience or, more accurately, an audience of those living in a situation where they <u>can</u> enjoy a retirement. But what about the "spiritual" in the title?

**"May this meditation be for the spiritual
awakening of all sentient beings."**

This dedicatory prayer is often uttered at the end of Buddhist meditation sessions. It is meant to both remind the meditator of his or her desire (ideally) to achieve enlightenment *in order to* benefit others, and to activate something like grace or an energy, which actually works to achieve the desired effect.

But this book is <u>not</u> a treatise on Buddhism. Rather, I reference that practice only in order to focus on the notion of "spiritual awakening". What could that mean? And is there any support for the notion that such a thing (a "spiritual awakening") actually exists? Which depends, of course, on what you think 'spiritual' means. And that <u>does</u> bring us to the subject of this book: <u>A Spiritual Guide for Retirement</u>. For here also, we need to determine what 'spiritual' means if we are going to say anything intelligent and practical.

And that, "what 'spiritual' means", turns out to be a wonderfully and perhaps surprisingly complex question. Not initially, I admit. Initially, there seem to be only a couple of main claimants for what the term means. But as we delve into these differing views, we'll come upon some intriguing, provocative and very rich other claims that are either presumed or implied by whichever meaning of 'spiritual' one adopts. And that can be very exciting and perhaps challenging, even daunting and maybe a bit fearsome. But hey, . . . you're retired now, you've got the time, have some 'fun'!

What we'll find as we get into the different meanings of 'spiritual' is an interesting debate or dialogue between two main views. One rooted firmly and unapologetically in the western, scientific and empirical camp and the other rooted just as firmly in a more universal, religious and experiential camp. And as we get into this dialogue or debate between these two views, we'll discover that each one relies on certain basic, fundamental *assumptions* to support their view of things. Assumptions that are so basic and fundamental they function as axioms or foundational beliefs in their respective belief systems. And these differing sets of assumptions ultimately cannot be reconciled.

Though most of the time these differing assumptions do not cause conflict in how we live our lives or view the world, there does come a time when a choice must be made. This book attempts to provide some grounds for making that choice. Grounds that take those foundational beliefs into account but <u>do not</u> depend on a resolution of their respective truth values, at least not in any typically logical or philosophical manner.

This then will be a journey of discovery. And, like most such journeys, it can be worrisome and exciting and a challenge. You're likely to come across beliefs that you never focused on before and now find that you *have to* hold them (believe them true) <u>IF</u> you're going to hold still other beliefs which you do indeed hold as true. And you may not be so sure you want to subscribe to those new beliefs. Or you may experience a kind of epiphany, a feeling that: 'a haa, I see it now, how it can all fit together, . . . and I like that whole. It "makes sense," it seems right to me.'

As you can now see, this book is not going to be a "self-help" book in the usual sense. There'll be no lists of "five things to see and do" or "4 habits to acquire in your spare time". Rather, it's more like a trail guide for a journey through some new and unexplored territory. You might think of it as a hike up a mountain trail. Your guide will keep you from falling or taking too dangerous a path or missing any of the spectacular views, but it will take some effort on your part.

For those who are intrigued enough to take the journey, a word or two to help you along the way. There are numerous sections embedded in the main text that play the role that a hyperlink does when you are on the web. In this book, however, these passages are simply indented and in a slightly smaller, but hopefully still readable, font size (11 pt vs. the 12 pt of the main text). They are further and fuller commentary on some point just made in the main text. They can be skipped without losing the train of thought or missing any major point. They are included only for those who might want to consider a particular point in more detail.

Most of the chapters are quite short, fewer than 10pp. and the book divides into two main sections, Parts I and II, including Ch's 1-5, and Parts III and IV, including Ch's 6-12. Despite the shortness of the book (barely more than 150 ? pp.) I do not envision anyone just sitting down and reading it straight through. Indeed, I would warn against trying to do so. Blurred vision and headaches might ensue. (I'm joking, I'm joking . . . . . . maybe.)

****

Spoiler Alert:

This book doesn't arrive at anything startlingly new. It's the way we get there and what we see along the way that's new. The view from the mountaintop is the same. But the way up and what we see along the way is different.

ACKNOWLEDGMENTS

I owe a great debt of gratitude to the many people who have helped me write this book. Most proximately, Karin Ringheim, Joe and Marlene McCarthy, Mary Morrow-Box, Tom Merrick, Ed Janus, Rick Langer and Steve McClure, all of whom read and commented on parts or all of the manuscript for this book. Their comments and criticisms were almost always helpful and thought provoking. And any fault that remains, is solely of my own doing.

More remotely, I owe a great debt to the many authors, living and dead, that I have had the opportunity and the privilege to read and ponder. Of great importance as well have been the many teachers, colleagues and friends who have been willing, sometimes even eager, partners in discussion and debate over these last sixty five years or so.

And a large debt is owed to the many students I have had over the years, especially during the last twelve years of my teaching career. I spent those years at a university engaged in what is often called continuing education. Most of the students were adults with full-time jobs and families who were attending school in addition to their many other responsibilities. Not only were they willing to engage in the many discussions we had, but they forced a clarity and plain-speaking as well as a relevance to their lives that is often missing in the higher reaches of academe.

And finally, but certainly not least, to my wife, Karin, for her support and encouragement especially throughout the long writing process. It would have been much more difficult without that encouragement and support.

PART I

CONTEXT AND GOAL

CHAPTER 1

<u>Now, You DO Have Time to "Smell the Roses"</u>

How often have we heard that admonition? Usually prefaced with: "be sure to take the time to . . ." And it's almost universally acknowledged to be sane and wise advice. Sane and wise advice throughout our lives to be sure, but even more appropriate, it is thought, during our retirement years. Indeed, some might even see it as <u>the</u> <u>main</u> <u>task</u> to be accomplished during those retirement years. Or, if that sounds too task-oriented for retirement, at least the main way to be spending one's time during retirement.

But as most often conceived, I will argue, it is too passive and too focused simply on the sensually enjoyable. Now, there's absolutely nothing wrong with the sensually enjoyable, but I think there is a more dynamic and much fuller way of conceiving this admonition. A way which does not stint on the enjoyable but envisions an even fuller and more satisfying life than one spent simply trying to appreciate and enjoy the beautiful that we happen to encounter in our lives. And, as a bonus, a way of conceiving this "smell the roses" such that it fits in much better with what we, ideally, have been doing in our lives up to the time of retirement. Fits in with, enhances and completes what we, again ideally, have been doing all along. The rest of this chapter will try to spell out that fuller and more active understanding of "smell the roses".

The very first and most obvious meaning of "smell the roses" has already been referred to above. Enjoy, appreciate and relish *the beautiful*. Take the time and put in the effort to really see and hear, smell, taste and feel what is around us. From the natural at its grandest: the ocean, the sky, deep space, vistas, sunlight and rainstorms to the particular: your own garden, the flowers on the table, the music on your play list, the wonder and laughter of your grandchild or the warmth and companionship of your pet dog (or cat).

Note that this is not to deny that there are horrendous things happening in the world. Disease, pestilence, wars, accidents, calamities of nature, man's cruelty to man, the list goes on. Rather it counsels us to recognize that there is also much beauty to be experienced and relished and enjoyed. And whereas the bad that happens around us and sometimes to us seems to impose itself on our consciousness, to demand our attention, the beauty that is there is all too often taken for granted, not even or barely seen or heard, smelled or touched.

Perhaps that is because it actually is the more common occurrence, that which forms the taken-for-granted, always-there background against which and in which we experience our lives. Or it may be because it usually doesn't demand our attention the way that horrendous happenings do. It's there, but we have to make a conscious effort to attend and to appreciate and to enjoy it.

But whatever the reason, the advice is the same: *stop*, attend, appreciate, relish and enjoy the beautiful in all its forms. Somehow, doing so is not just enjoyable, somehow it is thought to be fulfilling. It makes for a richer, more fulfilled life. It opens our minds and hearts to others and to other values. It helps us appreciate the world and others in ways that are often missed in our work-a-day, pragmatic, goal-oriented, busy, hectic lives.

That notion of relishing, appreciating and enjoying the beautiful as somehow fulfilling, as somehow making more whole our life experience and even ourselves in the process, seems to almost be or be like an axiomatic belief. Few (any?) who have taken the time to experience such beauty would deny that it is enjoyable and beyond enjoyable, that they somehow feel more complete, ***more fully human*** for having had the experience.

To even speak of it as a belief seems odd. It's more like a conviction arrived at through experience. Granted, but that conviction when expressed as above becomes a belief. (Note: obviously not in any religious sense of the term 'belief'.) And that kind of grounding for a belief– one obtained through personal experience– will become important and significant later on in this book. For now, we can take it simply as an aside but one that foreshadows something important later on.

But there is more to having a rich human experience of life, to becoming "more fully human," than just enjoying, appreciating and relishing the beautiful. And there is more to it than that because there is more to us than simply the satisfaction of our senses and the satisfaction of some aesthetic sense. There is also our mind. And the mind is exercised, in part, by searching for what's true and fulfilled in finding it.

So another aspect of "smell the roses" is to search for the truth in whatever area and in all areas. And here too we could speak of enjoying, appreciating and relishing this search and whatever success we have in the search. The satisfaction that we experience from such a search and its occasional successes doesn't *feel* the same as that which we experience from the pleasure our senses provide upon experiencing the beautiful, but it does provide its own kind of pleasure and perhaps even more than that sensual experience of the beautiful, it results in a sense, a feeling, of fulfillment, of being more fully what you most truly are.

But what does retirement bring to this endeavor? For most of us (all of us?) it's something we've been doing all along, from the first moment we entered the world–– trying to comprehend, to understand, what is so, what is the case. So how is it any different now?

Well, in addition to having more time and leisure to perhaps pursue the truth in areas you hadn't before or in areas you were interested in but didn't have the time to pursue, your new status in life provides you with some unique benefits. You no longer have to spend your time in the work-a-day world of (usually) pragmatic, means-end calculations and analysis. It's a bit like having spent your working years designing and drawing advertisements and you're now free to design and draw whatever strikes your fancy.

There are other benefits as well that come from your new status. Your history and experience give you (at least the chance of) an ability to approach any search from a new and fuller perspective, from one that is more comprehensive, less narrow, less self-serving.

And finally, as we get older and freer of the demands of simple survival (our own and that of our dependents), it may be that we discover a different ordering of values in our lives. And that different ordering of values can lead to a different set of interests vis-à-vis any search for the truth that we engage in. In addition, it can lead to a different ordering of the truths we have arrived at, and that in itself provides a new perspective.

By now you may suspect where this is going. "Smell the roses," I have alleged, means enjoying and relishing the beautiful but it also means searching for the truth. Hmmm. Truth, and beauty. Is he now going to speak of goodness? The classical triumvirate then of Truth, Beauty and Goodness? (Yes, "he" is, but bear with me. There will be something new in this.)

For we are also, and eminently so, social beings. We're born in and we live and grow and find our enjoyment and our fulfillment largely within a social context. It doesn't just take a village to raise a child, it takes a 'village' for us to become most fully what we are and can be. And how we interact with others within that 'village' constitutes the good being spoken of here. To ignore that is to ignore a central part of what we are, of who we are.

Thus, "smell the roses" also involves doing some good. From the smallest scale, e.g. being kind to your next-door neighbor, to the grandest scale, e.g. giving billions to help eradicate ignorance, poverty and disease. Do some good. Acknowledge, honor and express this fundamental fact of our human existence: we are, in a different but important sense, all family. Of course, doing some good is not always so simple. Just figuring out what is the good thing to do can, in some circumstances, be quite complicated and complex. And then actually doing it can take courage, overcoming selfishness or desire or fear and involve enormous resolve. Still, the recognition that there is good to be done and the commitment to incorporating that into our lives is an important aspect of "smell the roses".

'Listen,' you might now be saying to yourself, 'I've been patient and open-minded up to now, but how on earth do you scrunch "do some good" into "smell the roses"? 'Give . . me. . a. . break!'

How indeed? And the answer, and maybe surprisingly so, is through pleasure or, more carefully, 'pleasure'. It's obvious in the case of, literally, smelling roses. Smelling the sweet fragrance of a flower does bring pleasure, a very obvious and immediate sensual pleasure. But coming to discover some truth you hadn't known before, especially in an area of interest to you, also brings pleasure. Not sensual pleasure to be sure, but a pleasure none-the-less. A sense of joy, the elation of a discovery, a feeling of "ah haa" as in "ah haa, now I see". A satisfaction in coming to a better, more comprehensive, understanding of something you're curious about. There genuinely is intellectual pleasure. It can come from solving a puzzle or a mathematics problem, discovering a new planet, seeing a logical entailment you had never seen before, coming to know some historical facts, . . . and the list goes on.

Indeed, there's an interesting intersection between the sensual pleasure derived from our sensual experience of the beautiful and the pleasure derived from our intellectual activity in discovering the truth. That intersection occurs in our experience of man-made beauty, in paintings, statuary, architecture, poetry, music, etc. In all of these, typically, the more we know of their creation and the people that made them, the fuller the pleasure we have when we experience them.

Finally, there is the pleasure we often experience when we do the "right thing". Indeed, this pleasure is so constant a companion of acting morally, compassionately, with kindness, that some have turned it into the very motivation for such activity and thus conclude, erroneously, that all acts are essentially selfish. But no, all acts are not selfish and yes, doing the right thing and also going beyond the obligatory and doing something good-but-not-obligatory do, often, bring a sense of pleasure. We feel good, happy with ourselves, a sense that "the world" is better and we have contributed to that.

But all these kinds of pleasure are different. Can they be what tie together these three activities: enjoying the beautiful, searching for the truth and doing some good? I would argue that they can and that they can *because* they share a common base in *why* they are pleasurable. They are pleasurable for us because, though in different ways, they resonate with and express our human nature at its fullest, at its best. They resonate with and express what it is to be most fully human or to live a fully human life. A life without any of these components would just have less good in it than what a normal human can experience and would want to experience. (Note that in this usage, 'good' is being used in a non-moral sense of the term; it refers to something of value, something worthwhile, which includes but is not limited to something that *ought* to be done or avoided.)

This notion that there is a "human nature", something that all humans share at least potentially and that defines, in part, what it is to be human can be and is debated. As is the notion that there is some particular way or ways in which this human nature most fully and most properly expresses itself. But I think the reader will find that both convictions (whether they be assumptions or conclusions) are behind or underlie virtually every conviction about or exhortation to lead "a better life". Whether it's an exhortation to go to school and get an education or simply to read widely and listen to music; to get more exercise or eat healthily; to expose yourself to varied experiences or not to harm others; to learn how to play well with others or the value and "rightness" of empathy, compassion and kindness. All of these assume and are targeted at becoming a "better", a "fuller" human being. And thus all of them assume there is such a thing (at least notionally) and that its parameters can be, at least approximately, specified.

This is why you need to be doing all three of the activities noted above if you are to most fully encompass "smell the roses". Each brings with it its own kind of 'pleasure'. But more importantly, each corresponds to and expresses a different but essential aspect of our human nature. To ignore or omit any one of them is to settle for a less fully human existence than you could have.

But of course, this is an ideal. And whether in your life before retirement or during retirement itself, there can be circumstances that hinder and limit our ability to pursue all three or any one of them for that matter to its fullest extent. Nevertheless, these are the sorts of goods where any realization of them is a benefit to and improves the well-being of, the person involved.

So, take the time to "smell the roses;" to enjoy and relish the sensually beautiful, but also to continue searching for what's true and certainly to do some good. And all three, when taken together, help you to realize your best, your fullest, human self. What better way than this to spend your retirement? Now you've got the time, the leisure and the means to focus on all three. In this sense, your retirement can itself be a flowering, a blossoming out into you becoming the best and fullest 'you' you can be. It needn't at all be a time for closing down, shutting off, coasting into inactivity and resignation, ending in decrepitude and resentment.

But what does this "smell the roses" business, even in this new and expanded way of conceiving it, have to do with the supposed, the promised, subject of this book– a *spiritual guide* for retirement? A lot. But for that we move on to the next chapter.

******

CHAPTER 2

On Becoming More "Fully Human"
Or
Realizing a More "Fully Human" Existence

So, one (and arguably the most obvious) meaning of "smell the roses" is, as we've already seen, simply: enjoy, appreciate and relish the sensually and intellectually beautiful. I don't know whether much more needs to be said about that aspect of retirement's project, either by way of explanation or by way of motivation. What it means to enjoy, appreciate and relish the beautiful seems pretty self-explanatory. And the motivation to engage in such activities seems both natural and self-reinforcing.

But I think more does need to be said about the justification offered earlier and alluded to in the title of this chapter. In Ch. 1, I claimed that all three of the activities of retirement encompassed in the phrase "smell the roses" found a common rationale in the notion of leading and (hopefully) achieving a "fully human life" or, at least, a life *more* fully human, a life where all the best that one could experience and achieve as a human being and as the particular human being you are, was striven for.

Obviously, this is a goal, an ideal, and is thus seldom actually achieved– certainly not in its fullness. But it does offer us a target to shoot for and a standard, a measuring stick by which to gauge how close we're coming, how well we're doing. And just as obviously, there are infinitely many variations on how people both pursue the goal and the degree(s) to which they accomplish it. Which raises the question: does that mean it is a purely subjective goal? A goal which can be filled-in or specified in _any_ way the individual desires?

Yes and no. "Yes" in the sense that it is <u>each individual's</u> goal. In that sense it is subjective, it is <u>this subject's</u> goal. It is also subjective in that each person's goal will have variations that reflect that individual's distinctive attributes and abilities and their relative strength or presence in that individual. But the answer is also "no" in the sense that what comprises that goal is not purely arbitrary. There are legitimate components in this goal and there are also illegitimate components. Thus, if A (say, developing one's mental capacities) is a legitimate component, then not-A (refusing or failing to develop one's mental capacities) could not also be a legitimate component. So, "no" this goal cannot be filled in in just *any* way the individual desires.

Why is that? Because this goal of being "fully human" is ultimately based on capacities that we actually do have as human beings, it's not just plucked out of thin air, imagined, contrived or made up. And those capacities and abilities have natural directions and end-points to their exercise. Thus, e.g., in the physical realm, the development of one's musculature so that one is able to survive, function and maintain health entails certain kinds of activities and ends in certain kinds of results. Sitting and doing nothing do not accomplish the development; the result is not to become a corporeal blob, a Jabba the Hut if you will. (Though Jabba might defend his/her physical condition on the grounds that he is, after all, not a human being.) Similarly in the intellectual realm, the point of our capacity to know is, among other things, to survive and function in our society. And this capacity is exercised by experiencing things, by reading, by being taught, by questioning and thinking. And the result is knowledge about the way things work and are. It is not accomplished, e.g., by closing oneself in a room and smoking opium.

Strange examples. Would anyone ever think otherwise? Perhaps not, but the point is that our abilities and capacities do have natural paths of development and expression. This seems so obvious it's a wonder why it need be said at all. But the reason is to support the claim that the goal of becoming "more fully human" is not a goal whose definition is purely arbitrary. Some things rightly count as expressing that goal and some do not.

On the other hand, there is an almost infinite variety in how that goal is realized within these limit constraints, both in the paths taken to get there and in the end result. And that variety needs to be acknowledged and respected. The point of the previous comments was simply that allowing anything, <u>any</u> way of acting and being human, does not respect that variety. This can be a hard combination of truths to hold simultaneously in one's mind: some things rightly count as expressing our humanity and our becoming "more fully human" and some things do not, but there is a great variety in the things that do count (as well as a great variety in the things that do not count).

So, exercising and fulfilling the abilities and capacities we have as human beings leads, it is thought, to a more fully human life and to a more enjoyable life. But there is more to this view of things than just our natural abilities and their exercise. There is also the notion of a balanced development of and a hierarchy among these abilities.

The recommendation for *balance* is classical and virtually universal. From the Delphic oracle's "nothing in excess" and Aristotle's ethics of virtue and "the golden mean" to Buddha's "the middle way" and, perhaps most persuasively, from what our own experience tells us when we encounter someone who has devoted almost their entire energy to doing one thing or becoming skilled in just one way. And it is often captured in platitudes like: moderation in all things. I have no intention of basing the advisability of balance on platitudes, but refer to them only to point out that the need for some balance in the development and exercise of our human abilities is widely accepted as a good thing.

This notion of balance and moderation is challenged, however, by the view that to become truly great at anything, you have to dedicate a great part of your life and time to it. So, e.g., becoming a great ballet dancer may well result in your not being as educated or even as physically healthy as you might have otherwise been. On the other hand, you have achieved greatness in one thing that is part of our aforementioned triumvirate. Is that worth any loss of balance? Another rather common example of such a loss of balance can come in the form of great artists (musicians, painters, sculptors) who sometimes seem, for the benefit of their art, to ignore the moral dimension of how one should treat other people. But again, does the result of their obsession (their art) justify or excuse their treatment of others? This is doubtless one of the areas where that variety we spoke of before in how a more fully human life is achieved comes into play.

As an example of the *hierarchy* among our human attributes, it is typically thought that our physical abilities as impressive as they can be and as enjoyable their exercise and fulfillment is, are not thought of as the highest expression of what it is to be human. There are also our psychological and emotional abilities, our intellectual abilities and our ability to see and act within a moral dimension. All of these are seen as essential components to expressing our humanity at its best, and some are seen as more important in expressing what's peculiarly human, what is distinctively human, than are others. Indeed, and it is just this feature that establishes the hierarchy. The functions and abilities that we share with most others in the animal kingdom are at the bottom of the hierarchy; the abilities that are apparently specific and unique to being human are at the top of the hierarchy. The bottom isn't bad, it's just not as important in realizing a more fully *human* life as are the abilities that distinguish the human from the non-human animal kingdom.

This notion of a "fully human life" or a "*more* fully human life" has played and continues to play an important part in our lives, often without our even being aware of it. Growing up, it stood as the goal to be achieved or, at least, striven for (though usually not explicitly articulated as such). It was and is often the standard by which projects in education and personal development are judged. But again, what does all this have to do with the subject of this book? What does this have to do with any "*spiritual guide* for retirement"?

They are related because of the hierarchy just mentioned. In that hierarchy of human abilities to be developed, enjoyed and appreciated, the intellectual, moral and aesthetic abilities or capacities are usually seen as being toward the top of the hierarchy. It is the exercise and fulfillment of those abilities that is seen as the best of what makes us distinctly human. And it is the exercise and fulfillment of those abilities that comprise the humanist notion of 'spiritual' which we'll explicate more fully in the next chapter.

A further reason for highlighting this notion of "*more* fully human" is that it connects our life <u>in</u> retirement with our lives <u>before</u> retirement. There is no (or should not be any) decisive break between our lives before retirement and our lives in retirement. Of course we are no longer working to earn money or, at least, need not be. (We've noted in the Introduction, that this book assumes a developed country perspective where people are actually able to retire from the need and demands of "earning a living".) There certainly is that difference and the differences in daily activity that follows from that difference. But it is presumed that underneath, so-to-speak, those daily activities we've been engaging in to earn our living, there was an assumed, a taken-for-granted, goal which established the larger and more dominant framework for our lives. Namely, the goal of becoming the "most fully human" person we could become. The most basic project/task we have been pursuing all along is still our most basic task: viz., becoming *more fully human*.

(Note that there are many alternative ways of describing this goal. To be 'happy', content, at peace, and fulfilled are just some of the words used; to be "a good person", kind, compassionate, and considerate are still others.)

So, it is the top of that hierarchy of activities which comprise being more fully human that brings us back to the subject of this book, for those sorts of activities just are the 'spiritual' in the humanist's vision of things. Developing, exercising, experiencing those aspects of a human life constitute, for the humanist, the 'spiritual' and are what makes us 'spiritual' beings.

And as we'll see, the religious believer, though they would not identify these activities and experiences as what is most properly 'spiritual', would nevertheless fully accept and value them as expressing the higher, the more valuable, the more distinctive qualities of what it is to be human. It's just that they would say that there is something beyond them that the humanist has failed to perceive or denies. The 'spiritual' in the most proper sense of that term, namely, our ability to experience, to know and to take part in a realm, a reality, beyond the physical and beyond even the purely intellectual and the aesthetic.

Is the religious believer right about that? Or is the humanist right, that no, there is nothing beyond the physical, nothing "transcendent" other than these intellectual, aesthetic and moral capacities and abilities we've just been discussing. I intend to explore that question in the remainder of this book, but first a few more words about these two different meanings for the word 'spiritual'.

It is worth pointing out, before we go on to those different meanings for the word 'spiritual" that two of those components to the "more fully human life" which we've discussed, are closely interrelated. "Doing some good" involves "searching for the truth" and what one discovers in doing the latter will have great effect on the former.

Suppose, for example, that we take a widely accepted understanding of "doing some good". That would certainly involve feeding the hungry, clothing the naked, housing the homeless, tending to the sick, etc. Generally, the sorts of activities described by the beatitudes. And we might expand it somewhat by saying: food, shelter, clothing, health care and education. Surely these are all things that are good for people.

But that, then, is something you're claiming is true, that those things *really are* good for people. So far, it's hard to imagine any serious disagreement over such a claim. We may disagree over the best way to provide these goods and, of course, whether and how they are provided will depend on the development and wealth of the society involved. But that they are good for people seems hard to disagree with.

What shall we say, then, of "the spiritual"? Buddhist meditation sessions are often closed with this little dedicatory prayer: "May this meditation be for the spiritual awakening of all sentient beings". beings". What does "spiritual awakening" refer to? What does it mean? Is it something that is good for people? And the search for answers to these questions just is a search for the truth, the truth in this area. So these two components of that "fuller human existence" are closely interrelated. "Doing something good" would certainly seem to involve the beatitudes or that broader rendition of them as in: food, shelter, clothing, health care and education. But what about "spiritual awakening"? We have yet to determine what that means and whether it is also good for human beings. All of which leads us to the next chapter where we begin to explore what the 'spiritual' might mean.

PART II

THE COSMOLOGY OF IT

CHAPTER 3

<u>Two Different Meanings of 'Spiritual'</u>

In my many talks with people over the last few years as I was thinking about this subject and book, I discovered that there are numerous different meanings that people assign to the word 'spiritual'. But there are just two that predominate.

The first of these is the obvious and expected, what I'll refer to as the *religious* spiritual. Here the speaker is referring to something totally non-physical and in that sense something transcendent. Usually such a meaning includes notions such as soul, an afterlife and God.

The second meaning commonly offered is a bit harder to describe but I'll refer to it henceforth as the *humanistic* meaning. Under this interpretation, the 'spiritual' refers to any human activity that expresses or experiences the so-called "higher" human attributes that we spoke of in the last chapter. So that the 'spiritual' in this sense involves, e.g., our appreciation of beauty, whether in poetry or music or art or nature or . . . It also includes our ability to empathize with and care for others, as well as our ability to conceive of and act on our conceptions of justice and fairness, right and wrong, good and evil. Under this interpretation, one is being 'spiritual' when one focuses on those aspects of our lives that extend beyond our purely physical needs and functions, e.g., our quest for food, shelter and clothing. Anything, any need and activity that we share with the rest of the animal kingdom would not be 'spiritual' in this sense. A 'spiritual' guide for retirement would, on this accounting, focus on the truth, beauty and goodness highlighted in the first chapter.

On some accountings, the Ethical Culture Society and the Unitarian Universalist Association (UUA) would be examples of organizations that would subscribe to this second meaning of 'spiritual'. (An important caveat to this claim is to note that neither group, to my knowledge, denies *the possibility of* something 'spiritual' in the first or religious sense noted above. Rather, and as organizations, they are agnostic on that issue and choose to focus instead on this second, the humanistic meaning of 'spiritual'. And even that claim would need to be modified with respect to the UUA. Their position seems more to be something like: 'we think there is a God, a supreme being of some sort, and our services will reflect that belief, but we're accepting of multifarious different ways of conceiving such an entity and are more than welcoming to those who choose not to believe in any such entity at all since our main focus is and will be on the ethical implications of our common humanity.'

People who think first (or exclusively) of this sense of 'spiritual' will often respond to a question like: "what does the spiritual mean to you?" with references to the feelings and emotions aroused in them by nature or art or music. As in, e.g., "listening to Beethoven's 9th just transports me to my spiritual side" or "I'll tell you what it means to me, it's what happens to me when I'm standing before Picasso's Guernica– the emotions, the thoughts it inspires; I'm transported into a different realm. That realm just is the 'spiritual' for me." And finally, "when I can see others and their needs as equally as important as my own, that's when I feel what I would call my 'spiritual' side."

Another common way of referring to the 'spiritual' in this tradition is to refer to "the human spirit". As in: attend to, nourish, love and support the "human spirit" in each of us. And presumably this "human spirit in each of us" refers to that part of us that strives for and wants to connect with others, to be honest with ourselves, to be the best person we can be, to survive and endure; yes, but also to flourish and, especially, to help others do the same.

So, two different meanings, at least two different <u>major</u> meanings for the term 'spiritual'. How, then, shall we proceed? Which of these will be the focus for this "spiritual guide for retirement"? Both will be. And both will be first, because those are the two major ways of understanding this term and this notion and it would be simply arbitrary to ignore either one of them. And, secondly, because ultimately they are not compatible, they cannot both be true in their starkest formulations. So it would seem that we must consider both to help us make the decision of which we want to ascribe to.

Note that by-and-large, the humanist's meaning can be subsumed into the religious meaning. There is nothing that the humanist meaning asserts or subscribes to that the religious meaning cannot endorse and accept, *except in one case.*

And that one case is when the humanist position is taken as exclusive and exhaustive. When it is taken as asserting not just that these higher human attributes, qualities and abilities and their exercise is a 'spiritual' experience but that it is <u>the only viable meaning</u> of 'spiritual', that any other meaning (e.g. the religious meaning briefly referenced above) is simply nonsense or betrays an infantile, absurd, childish and patently false position. In that case, obviously, that humanistic meaning cannot be subsumed into the religious meaning.

Going forward, I'll refer to the two different humanistic stances we've just surveyed as *the open humanist* position (OH for short) and *the secular humanist* position (SH for short). The open humanist position is the one which, in addition to holding that the 'spiritual' is commonly and most properly thought of as encompassing those "higher" human experiences referred to above, takes a "yet, it is possible that" or an agnostic approach to the religious meaning of 'spiritual'. In that sense it is open. And the classic example of such a stance in today's (American) society would be those that were mentioned earlier: the Unitarian Universalist Association and, possibly, the Ethical Culture Society.

The secular humanist position on the other hand will refer to a position that holds that any of the classically religious interpretations of 'spiritual' are mistaken and false in that what they are referring to by their use of the term 'spiritual' does not or even cannot exist.

To reiterate, there need not be any conflict between the open humanist meaning of spiritual and the religious meaning of that same term. Everything the humanist refers to as spiritual could be (indeed, not just could be, but usually is) accepted by a religious believer though the latter might contend that the more proper meaning of the term 'spiritual' is the transcendent meaning. Any dispute between them on this issue is merely verbal – a dispute about the best or most apt use of a linguistic term.

Not so between the secular humanist position and the religious position. As before, the religious believer is happy to endorse and subscribe to a spiritual quality in all of those "higher human attributes" and their exercise, which we've already spoken of, but is not willing to agree that there is no other sensible meaning for the term 'spiritual'. Here, any dispute is not merely verbal, for the one party holds that there are actual referents for the religious meaning of 'spiritual' while the other party holds that there are not and possibly even cannot be any such referents.

Then how shall we proceed? What is a spiritual guide for retirement to do with such a conflict? The attempt will be to resolve it or, at least, to show a way through it. This is the journey we'll be taking; the 'mountain' mentioned in the Introduction that we'll be trying to climb. And doing so falls perfectly within the open or even secular humanist agenda. For solving it, or attempting to solve it, just is an instance of searching for the truth, viz. the truth in this particular area. Thus, along with enjoying, appreciating and relishing the beautiful, and along with doing some good, we can be searching for the truth in this area. This combination would then fully implement "a spiritual guide for retirement" for either forms of the humanist meaning of 'spiritual'.

But it would also implement a spiritual guide for retirement for the religious believer. First because, as noted above, those activities of the classical triumvirate fall easily and entirely within the scope of the religious meaning of 'spiritual'. And secondly because the believer (and similarly for the secular humanist) is here faced with a contradiction. His position (that there is some transcendent reality) cannot be true if the secular humanist's position (there is nothing transcendent) is true. This challenge calls out for resolution, and does so equally for both sides. To the reflective, honest and open-minded searcher, it's not a challenge that can simply be ignored or set aside, at least not without first examining it and one's reasons for coming down on one side or the other.

This aspect of a life in retirement– examining the truth or falsehood of your position on the 'spiritual'– corresponds closely with the "forest dweller's" project, which was mentioned in the Introduction. There, as you will recall, the Hindu believer, having entered the "retirement stage" of life, took it as an opportunity to fully devote himself to examining, practicing and pursuing the meaning of existence as that had been presented to him throughout his life through Hindu teachings and beliefs. (As also noted in the Introduction, this whole approach to retirement seems to have been (and be?) specifically for the *male* Hindu. And that, as you can well imagine, raises all sorts of problems and points of discussion, which we won't get into here.) In that tradition, if he was successful, if he succeeded in realizing the meaning of existence, he returned to the work-a-day world of daily life a changed man, now living as a *sannyasin*, a wandering mendicant and ascetic. Someone who could now be in the world but not be induced or swayed by its blandishments and entreaties away from his goal of realizing his oneness with Brahman. The *sannyasin* is sometimes described as one who neither loves nor hates anything. Which has its echoes in Buddhism and that practitioner's efforts to free himself from both attachment and aversion.

> (At first glance, this 'neither loving nor hating anything' does not seem to be a very attractive or desirable way of being. But an exegesis of the concept is neither necessary for our purposes here nor appropriate. For anyone interested, I would direct them to any of various texts on comparative religions.)

But we are not Hindus, so (and even for most Hindus) the goal is not to become a *sannyasin*. Nor need the search require going off to some secluded spot and spending years in isolation and deprivation. We are (or are soon going to be) in retirement. We feel we have earned and want to enjoy some leisure, we want to "smell the roses" in all the dimensions we've already talked about. And that is not a problem. It is perfectly compatible with this search for the truth. Indeed, I would argue that it actually helps it. It keeps the search grounded in our lives for we would want whatever answer we come up with to fit in with the whole range of our activities, beliefs and values.

Part of this "Guide for Retirement," then, will concern itself with looking at this particular conflict between the religious meaning of 'spiritual' and the secular humanist meaning. 'Ahhhhhh,' you might be saying to yourself about now. 'Despite the title, this is not your usual "Self Help" book.' And, as I also said in the Introduction, you would be right about that, it is not. On the other hand, it's not going to be a textbook in philosophy either. I will not proceed by mounting logic-book arguments for one side and then the other. Rather, I'll spend some time trying to get clear about what each side is saying, what they are claiming is so. And then, the fun part, seeing what each of those major claims or positions either implies or assumes, or both.

It is often enlightening to walk through such an examination. For you may not always be aware of what is implied by your own stance on a particular subject or what it assumes as an unexamined, background, given. And once those implications and assumptions become clear, it often throws your original position into a whole new light. Suddenly you may think: "Whoa! Really? If that's the case (if X is *implied by* what I'm saying or believing, or what I'm saying or believing *assumes* that Y is the case), then I'm not so sure I want to hold on to it."

That can be exciting. But it can also be daunting, even fearful and certainly unsettling. And that does not seem to be very desirable fare for this stage of retirement, so why would one engage in it?

Well, first of all, recall that this is not the only thing you'll be doing in retirement. There are also those elements of enjoying the beautiful and doing some good. Both of which will help to keep you sane and grounded, . . . and enjoying this time. But beyond that, there should be a rock bottom assurance and peace in the conviction that finding out what's true (even just searching for it) cannot be bad, and trying to live one's life in accordance with that truth should lead to a harmony and to happiness. In this regard, most religious traditions echo the biblical admonition: "you shall know the truth and the truth shall set you free."

But discovering what's true is seldom if ever a straight-line or a quick and simple event. There are many false turns and dead ends along the way. And to be morose or, let's face it, just realistic for a minute, suppose you have gone down one of those dead ends or made a false turn on this journey of discovery and then die? Die before discovering what really is the case? Aye, suppose you do? Could you have been doing anything better as an alternative? What? Refusing to look? Not undertaking the journey? Consciously deciding that you'll rest in your current convictions without further examination? Isn't that a bit like deciding to just coast through the remainder of your time until you die? There is pleasantness to that, I suppose, little effort, no strain, no stress. (Well, no stress only if you can suppress the niggling: 'but suppose I'm wrong? Suppose I haven't got it right?')

But maybe you "have it right". Maybe there are no "niggling doubts" unsettling your peace. You're content that you've found the truth in this area. In that case, this approach may not be the one for you. Though it may still be interesting to peruse just by way of checking to see if there's anything you may have missed.

Finally, because the open humanist position referred to above, is not incompatible with and can even be subsumed into the religious spiritual position, in the next chapter I'll be focusing on the secular humanist position, the humanist position which, in the end, is incompatible *with* the religious spiritual take on things.

******

CHAPTER 4

<u>The Secular Humanist 'Spiritual' and</u>
<u>Its Assumptions or Implications</u>

The first thing to note is that the "secular humanism" I am referring to here is, in essence, a materialism. It is sometimes also referred to as naturalism. It holds that there is nothing other than the physical or whatever is caused by, or is dependent upon, the physical. Thus, it denies that there is anything like a supernatural realm, nothing spiritual in the religious sense of that term, nothing transcendent in that sense.

But please note that the "secular" in the title to this chapter does <u>not</u> mean that the position referred to represents or implies a materialistic *character* in the person who holds such a position. It is not, e.g., saying that any such person is someone who is only interested or primarily interested in acquiring things or stuff. Rather, it is referring to a humanism that asserts that there are particular limits to what can or does exist and to the kinds of things we can know. Those limits define barriers beyond which, according to these humanists, there is nothing or, at least, beyond which nothing can be known. Thus, such humanism denies any kind of entity other than material or physical entities and whatever such entities cause to exist. In addition, it is closed to ways of coming to know anything other than by way of the scientific method. This latter position is sometimes referred to as scientism. (Though to be entirely fair, I should perhaps have put the word "know" above in scare quotes to indicate that the humanists holding such a position may be referring to a very specific kind of or degree of knowing when they make this claim.)

Now as we have learned from science over the last hundred years or so, the "physical" or "matter" is not so easy to define. Or, perhaps better, there are entities that we're pretty sure do exist but do not meet all the criteria of the more commonsense definitions of matter, or the physical. A common definition of matter, e.g., might be: whatever has mass, whatever can cause a gravitational reaction. We also think of anything physical, or material, as having a spatial location and shape and of having parts or being able to be broken into parts. But once we get into the whole array of subatomic particles, energy waves, indeed even energy itself, things get murky. Do electrons have mass? Do protons and neutrons have a shape? And what about the proton's components, quarks? Are they matter or material? If not, how can they comprise something that is?

> A critical and important realization that affects our discussion is that the very notion of the material or the physical has undergone (and is undergoing) massive changes within the scientific community. And these changes may cause a sea change in the framework of this discussion. If we don't understand what energy and matter are or the manners of existing that each can assume, this whole debate may be misguided or even "a red herring". It may be based on an outmoded and too simplistic a view of the distinction between the physical and the spiritual.
>
> As an example of such changes in the conception of matter: we have gone from Newtonian physics with matter as composed ultimately of *little billiard ball entities* subject, at some level, to gravity and existing independently of any observer, to relativity theory and matter existing in relation to the position and movement of the observer, to the wave-particle duality of quantum mechanics, where only one of these features can manifest at any given time and where such manifestation is dependent upon a viewer, a consciousness, deciding what it is interested in knowing, and finally, to matter existing as *a probability wave* that is defined by way of mathematical equations.

And to the degree this change in understanding of matter is the case, it seems to be moving in the direction of less deference to, less dependence upon, something with mass, shape or color as the foundational 'stuff' from which everything else is made. It seems to be moving in the direction of something transcendent, something not material in the classical sense, something that does not display any of the classical physical properties we are familiar with in our common, daily experience. For example, the probability wave we just spoke of. In addition, it is claimed that it is part of our common, daily experience even if it is not recognized or experienced as such. And that such "transcendence" is actually inseparable from matter (in its classical definition). But I will leave that approach and analysis to someone else and to some other time to pursue.

There is another variation on this same theme of the meaning of 'matter', which is worth at least pointing out. It is the view that does not deny that something non-physical exists, e.g. thoughts, memories, images, feelings, etc., or even consciousness itself and maybe some form of ultimate reality. Rather, it would say, these entities **all** *emerge from* **matter**, or from 'matter'. They are there from the very beginning in some inchoate form, but once they emerge, they are genuinely distinct from matter but still dependent upon it for their existence. In this way, it is thought to avoid the matter- non-matter, or the matter - spiritual (in the religious sense) duality.

This approach might solve the problem of the apparent difference and incompatibility of the material and the spiritual (in their classical meanings), but it does so by massively changing the traditional concept of matter. On this view, 'matter' comprises everything from stones and trees to thoughts and consciousness and God. It "solves" the problem but does so only by a verbal sleight-of-hand. And, I would submit, it does so at a very abstruse and wholly intellectual level. As lived, the problem persists for most people and, as we get older, becomes even more insistent. Is this all there is? Is there, at the end of our earthly existence, simply nothing or is there something else *for us*?

One way around these complications about the territory covered by the term 'matter' or the range of things that are to be included in its domain is to approach the question in a different way, through epistemology; i.e. by way of what we can know or how we come to know anything. With this approach, one might define the material or the physical as whatever can be accessed by our senses or any of their technological extensions, like microscopes and telescopes or even an electroencephalograph or a cloud chamber.

These latter two examples of extensions of our senses raise a third possibility for defining the material or the physical since in both these cases, you're not seeing the thing itself being measured, rather you're seeing the effect it has on a measuring instrument. Thus in these cases we might say that something is physical only if it can cause a physical effect. Or we might say: whatever is susceptible of being tested by means of the scientific method is physical or material.

But finally, I'll end this little side commentary on the meanings of 'matter' by mentioning the eminent 20th century physicist and Nobel Laureate Richard Feynman's comment that "in physics today, we have no knowledge of what energy is". And if energy and matter are mutually transformable ($E=mc^2$), then we would also have no knowledge of what matter is. "No knowledge" in either case might be a bit strong. Maybe we'd be better off saying: we do not fully understand what either is.

But all of the various efforts to clarify what the "material" is complicate beyond our scope here any attempt to determine whether there is anything spiritual in the religious sense. Either their range becomes unclear at its extreme or they beg important questions in the current debate. To actually progress in our inquiry, we may have to leave the definition a little fuzzy or, at least, avoid trying to settle the hard cases. For the remainder of this book, then, I'll take it that the material, the physical, is whatever has mass, size or shape and is accessible to our senses or their extensions.

To repeat then, the secular humanist's position is that there is nothing other than the physical or the material, and whatever is caused by, or is dependent upon, the material for its existence.

And if they are right, it would certainly rule out anything claimed to exist in the strictly religious meaning of 'spiritual' since God, souls and an afterlife, as commonly conceived in the religious context, are definitely thought of as not being material or physical, nor in any essential way dependent upon anything material or physical for their existence.

So one question that presents itself is: *why* does the secular humanist hold the position she does? And why, often, with such certainty? In an effort to answer or at least begin to explore this question, I would like to eavesdrop on a little dialogue between a secular humanist (SH) I'll call Sue, and, for want of a more mellifluous term, a religious spiritualist (RS) I'll call Tom.

****

RS OK, Sue, I think I understand <u>what</u> you're saying but I'm still not clear about *why* you think that it is so. <u>Why</u> do you think that there is nothing other than the physical or the material, and whatever is caused by the physical or material? [I'll use these two terms interchangeably from here on to avoid the clumsy phrasing.]

SH   Well, I guess I'd start with: because no one has ever been able to show me anything or, to avoid an obvious begging of the question, convince me that there is anything which both exists and is <u>not</u> physical.

RS   Really? What about your own thoughts and memories, your imaginings, attitudes and even feelings (like love, anger etc.)? Aren't those 'things' that clearly exist but are not physical? They don't have any mass or shape or color or size.

SH   Well, certainly as we experience them, in our subjective experience of them, they don't have any physical characteristics. But, I would contend, they are all, nevertheless <u>caused by</u> and dependent upon processes in the brain, processes that <u>are</u> physical.

RS   You know, actually, we don't really know that. All we know is that there seems to be a close correlation between various different kinds of brain events and our subjective experiences of mental events, thoughts, images, memories and the like.

SH   Well yes, technically I think that's all we ever know about any claimed causal connection isn't it? Hume's famous "constant conjunction". So yes, such a constant conjunction between a brain event and a subjective experience of a certain sort does *not prove* that the brain event *causes* our subjective experience of that brain event, but it seems like awfully good evidence for it. Especially so when you add in the fact that we can disrupt, change or even destroy, seemingly, such subjective experiences of mental events by physically or chemically altering the brain.

RS Except maybe not. Maybe that close correlation reflects instead a connection that's necessary only if we are to *express* our subjective mental experiences in our embodied state. Similar to the way various neuronal firings in the brain are apparently required if we are going to express a welcome greeting to another by raising our hand in a wave of hello.

SH What!??

RS In other words, the correlation is there, but it points to a different kind of dependency. It's not that the brain events cause the mental events, but rather that the brain events enable <u>our expression of</u> the mental events. The brain events enable us to speak the words, or smile or raise our hand or even the "light" in our eyes. In this view of things, think of the brain as a radio receiver, our consciousness and its contents as the radio waves, and the mechanics within the radio receiver as the axons and dendrites within our brain. If the mechanics within the radio receiver don't work then the radio receiver won't be able to convert the radio waves into discernible and intelligible sound for us the listener. Similarly, if the neuronal components and connections within our brains don't work properly then we won't be able *to express* our thoughts and the other contents of our consciousness.

SH Well . . . . Interesting. But if that's so, then what causes the brain events?

RS In this analysis, it would be the mental events themselves. They would be like the radio waves. Thus, for example, the mental event *of wanting* to speak or wave causes the brain event of certain neuronal firings.

SH Woah! Are you serious?

RS   What I'm saying is it's possible, it *could* be this way. This description of how things work is perfectly compatible with the physical facts of the case. Now, I'll certainly grant you that this "could be" does not prove that the brain event is not actually causing our subjective experiences, but it does show that there is an alternative explanation for the same set of facts. An explanation that seems, on its face, to be equally plausible.

SH   No, I disagree. Maybe equally *possible*, but I do not think equally *plausible*.

RS   Well . . . . I don't know about that. I can think of cases where this way of conceiving of things actually seems to fit the facts better.

SH   Really? Like what?

RS   Like people who are in comas, apparently totally unaware and certainly unresponsive to whatever is going on around them, unable to communicate in any way with others and yet, when they awaken from the coma, both claim and are able to demonstrate that they were fully aware during much of the time and maybe even had an active mental life going on. In fact, they were maddeningly frustrated by their inability to communicate to anyone their conscious awareness.

Now admittedly, we don't know in such cases whether their inability to communicate is due to brain malfunction or to some one or other somatic malfunction. But the distinction between consciousness and its contents apparently being separable from brain events is at least provocative.

But let me set aside, for now, this claim that the hypothesis that mental events may cause the brain events seems to actually fit the facts of some of our human experience better than does the alternative view, the view that brain events cause mental events. Let's set that aside for now and simply say that either one is equally *possible*. Then, is there any good reason for preferring one to the other? Any good reason for thinking that one is the truth of the matter? Any reason, that is, that does not just beg the question?

SH Ahh ha! And if I say 'because everything that exists just is material or physical', you'd say that I'm begging the question.

RS And so you would be, yes?

SH Well, how about: because this way of thinking, of approaching our understanding the world, viz. through science and the scientific method, has proven so informative and useful, especially over the last 400 years or so, that we would be foolish to abandon it in this case.

> [Where "scientific method" refers explicitly, precisely and only to: the formulating and testing of *empirically* testable hypotheses. And *empirical* here means: simultaneously accessible to objective, third party observation (or other sensory stimulation).]

RS Ahhhh. Tempting, but I think it still just begs the question. And it does so by trading on the ambiguity in the word 'world'. If you mean by "the world", the physical universe, then in counseling that we restrict ourselves to the scientific method in the study of our own consciousness and its contents, e.g., you are indeed assuming what is to be proven, viz. that our own conscious subjective experiences just are physical or caused by the physical. That would indeed and again be begging the question.
If, on the other hand, you want to use 'world' more expansively, to encompass everything that exists (or might exist), then it's not

clear that the scientific method is the only or even the best way to go in all cases.

SH What are you saying? That because something other than the physical *might* exist, we should not restrict our means of knowing purely to the methods of science?

RS Yes. That is, we should not *apriori* (before waiting for all the evidence to come in) restrict our possible ways of knowing. But I think there are even stronger arguments against such a restriction.

SH Such as?

RS Such as that we already do so in some areas of our lives and in our pursuit of knowledge. I.e. we already do not restrict our means of knowing to purely scientific means.

SH Like where?

RS Well, mathematics for one. The laws of logic for another. In both of these cases, we come to know the truth of what is asserted or claimed, not by using our senses or any extension of them, but in some other way(s). Some have called it intuition.
And to get really philosophical about your position for just a minute, the truth of the claim that: "the only valid, reliable knowledge is that which is obtained through using the scientific method" cannot itself be shown to be true by using the scientific method. Thus, it is a self-defeating claim.

SH Woahhhh. I thought we were having a friendly little discussion here?

RS I know, I know, I'm sorry. But I do think it's important to realize that being open to other ways of coming to know something

—ways other than the methods of science— does not depend solely on the fact that non-physical entities *might* exist. Those methods of science don't even cover subjects that clearly do exist and that we engage with every day (e.g. mathematics, logic and one's own subjective states). So being "open" to these other ways of knowing is basically just being realistic, ... and honest.

SH   OK, but would you agree, at least, and based on your examples of mathematics and the laws of logic, that we could (and should?) say that these so-called 'things', these non-physical entities, if they exist at all, *exist* in a different way than do the objects of our senses?

RS   Yes, absolutely. Though it's not a totally different meaning of the word 'exist'. I would argue that there are some similarities or commonalities in its use in each case, but there are clearly also some differences.
But back to our original question Sue, and why you are so committed to the physical or material (and whatever they might cause) as being the only reality that actually exists.

SH   Well, I think I have indicated why. And it seems to me that the best you've been able to come up with is that something non-physical and not caused by the physical – *might* exist. I'll grant you that. It doesn't seem to be a logical impossibility, but why go beyond that? Let me put the burden back on you, why do you think that anything other than the physical <u>actually does</u> exist?

******

From this little dialogue, we can see that the main assumptions of the SH are:

(1) **There is nothing other than the physical and whatever is caused by the physical. (materialism / naturalism)**

(2) **Only the physical can interact with something physical.**

(3) **The only reliable knowledge that one can obtain is that which is obtained through science and the scientific method. (Scientism)**

Well yes, you might say, Sue took these positions, but why call them "assumptions"?

Because, as we've just witnessed in this dialogue, any argument initially proposed to establish them, ultimately came down to simply asserting what was to be shown, viz. that the physical or what is caused by the physical is all that exists. Or, that the scientific method is the best (the only?) way of coming to know anything and it has been so successful over the past 400 years at unveiling the mysteries of *the physical* universe.

Though any arguments Sue gave were either logically defective or inconclusive, they did reveal her reasons for holding the position and the reasons she gave <u>are</u> common ones. They are, I think, the reasons or at least the kinds of reasons that most everyone would give in support of those positions: common sense, plausible reasons. It's only when one tries to turn them into sound arguments that they fail to carry the weight they were designed to carry.

But as we'll see in the next chapter, the religious spiritualist position is similar in this regard; it has its own "assumptions" as well.

CHAPTER 5

<u>The Religious Spiritual and Its Assumptions or Implications</u>

[Reader warning: this chapter is longer than most, a bit more complex and has numerous indented commentaries. All of which makes it harder to take in at one sitting. I would recommend a first reading of just the major text to get the lay of the land. Then, if you're so inclined, go back and enjoy the further commentaries.]

The religious meaning of 'spiritual' in this context will refer to any meaning that claims or posits something transcendent, something that exists but is not material or physical and is not dependent upon the physical or material for its existence. And in that sense, something that transcends the physical world we are all familiar with. Candidates for such a something are things like the soul, spirits (angels and demons), God, and possibly heaven or an afterlife. And most commonly (among virtually all religions), but interpreted variously: some form of ultimate reality, something from which, supposedly, everything else comes and on which everything else depends. In the three Abrahamic religions, this ultimate reality is identified as Yahweh, or God or Allah and given a personality. In the major Eastern religions, Hinduism and Buddhism, this ultimate reality (Brahman in Hinduism and Dharmadhatu in Buddhism) is not usually endowed with any personal characteristics. In classical texts on comparative religion, such a non-personal ultimate reality is often referred to as a "Godhead" rather than a God.

> Note: throughout the remainder of this chapter (and book) I will often use and refer to Buddhism in the examples I use of the religious spiritual. And this choice requires two, brief, comments. The first has to do with Buddhism

itself. There are many schools, interpretations and lineages within the Buddhist tradition and therefore what I adduce in some particular instance as "the" Buddhist position on an issue will almost certainly not accord in all respects with all of these different lineages or interpretations. But since no one of these traditions, lineages and interpretations is considered canonical, the best I can do is to simply indicate the one I will be using in this work. I will be speaking in terms of The Great Perfection (Dzogchen) tradition of Tibetan Buddhism.

The second point of explanation has to do with using Buddhism rather than Christianity as a main source of examples in this discussion. And the reasons are both personal and, hopefully, helpful. Though I come originally from the Christian tradition, I have been investigating Buddhism and practicing Buddhist meditation for the last 25 years or so and therefore it is most "at the front of" my mind when it comes to trying to understand and explicate these issues. And the helpful reason is simply the hope that speaking in terms of a Buddhist tradition rather than the Christian or other Abrahamic traditions some one of which, I suspect, most of my readers will share, may give the reader a fresher and less predisposed perspective from which to consider these topics.

To briefly review, in the last chapter we inquired why the "secular humanist" (Sue in the dialogue) rejected the reality of anything spiritual in the religious sense of the term, anything spiritual in the sense of something that exists but is neither material nor dependent upon the material for its existence. And what we saw was that any arguments she adduced to support her position ended up begging the question. What we discovered was that she brought to the discussion and to that effort of support and defense, a set of beliefs and conditions which, when taken together, ruled out from the beginning any possibility of something non-material existing. (Though she later conceded the *possibility* of such.)

Her argument went as follows: 'well, it's obvious that something physical exists and not at all obvious that anything non-physical exists, and since the only way we can *know* anything about what exists is through our senses (the empirical methods of science), we can conclude that either nothing beyond the physical exists or, if it does, we can't know about it'. But of course, if you restrict what can and does exist to what can be known only via the senses and their extensions, you will have won your case. But you will have won it only by assuming what you needed to show. A metaphysical claim (a claim about what does or can exist) is supported by an epistemological claim (about the only way we can know anything) which itself simply asserts that we can't 'know' anything beyond the physical.

And now we ask: is the religious spiritualist in any better position? Let's see. The question for the religious spiritualist, then, would be what Sue ended the previous dialogue with: what reasons do you (the RS) have for thinking that something neither material nor dependent upon the material for its existence, actually does exist?

We've already seen (in the dialogue in Ch. 4) the reference to subjective mental events as examples of 'things' that exist but are not material. Ideas don't have mass or size, weight or color. But mightn't they be caused by something that does, something that is material, viz. the brain? The religious spiritualist argued (in the dialogue) that there was no proof that they were. There is often demonstrable *correlation* between neuronal brain events and subjective mental events, but correlation does not prove causation. On the other hand, the possibility of there being such a causal relation could not be ruled out either. So we were left with: subjective mental events are not themselves material entities, but they *may be* caused by and dependent upon a material entity, viz. the brain.

More practically, however, most religious spiritualists would not start with subjective mental events as the reason for their belief that something 'spiritual' in the transcendent sense, actually exists. They would start with such things as: the way they were raised, the culture they grew up in, tradition, the training/teaching they received growing up and/or by referencing one or more "sacred" or "revealed" texts.

And though these are no doubt accurate accounts of how they actually did come to believe what they believe, we can still ask: but do any of these experiences constitute a good *reason* for such a belief? I.e. for thinking that the belief is true. (And remember we are here talking about the one particular belief that underlies everything else they believe in this context, viz. that there is indeed something transcendent, something that exists which is neither material nor dependent upon the material for its existence.

Without being dismissive of or denigrating any of the experiences just mentioned, I think it is pretty clear that "the way you were raised", "the culture you grew up in", "tradition", or "the teaching or training you received growing up" are none of them any evidence for the truth of what you believe. To establish the truth of any claim, you have to look at the evidence for the claim itself, not at the provenance from which it came. And this is true whether that provenance is a Buddhist monastery, an Islamic madrasa or a Christian Sunday school.

The "sacred" or "revealed" texts justification presents a somewhat different challenge but, as it turns out, will prove to be equally wanting as evidence for the truth of the belief we are examining here.

The problem with depending on any "sacred" text as evidence for the spiritual is demonstrated by the question: but why believe the "sacred" text? Typically, the answer comes back either: because the "sacred" text itself claims it is trustworthy or because someone whose position and authority themselves depend on the "sacred" text being the truth, claim that it is so.

But for either of those to be a good *reason* for believing the "sacred" text to be revealing the truth, one would need to first believe or have *independent* grounds for thinking that the source, S, knew what he, she or it was talking about. One would need to have *independent* grounds for thinking the source (the text itself or the person representing the text) was reliable; i.e. grounds independent of the very text or source of authority they are promoting. Otherwise, one is in the unenviable position of arguing:

(1) I believe that X (some claim about the way things are) because this text tells me it is so; and

(2) I believe this text because the text itself assures me it is revealed or sacred or trustworthy. (And if not the text itself, then someone who teaches the text and, typically, whose status and position depends on the text being taken as truthful, tells me it is so.)

In other words, one would have to depend on an obviously circular argument. And circular arguments don't work, they fail to support what they are alleged to support.

An experience of the transcendent.

But what about **an experience of the transcendent**? Would <u>that</u> provide reasonable evidence that such exists? Within the Buddhist tradition, e.g., it is thought that one can have the same kind of experience the Buddha had when he experienced awakening or enlightenment under the Bodhi tree. Not only does the classic 8-fold path of Buddhism imply as much, but also the Buddha's own exhortations to his followers imply or say as much outright. And included in those exhortations was his very explicit instruction not to believe simply because he had said it, rather he exhorted them: 'don't believe this because I'm saying it, but go out and do what I have done, go out and experience it for yourselves'.

45

Now admittedly, it may be and has been disputed whether Buddha's awakening involved anything transcendent, but certainly the Dzogchen tradition leans strongly in that direction. (Indeed, even the most classical interpretation of *nirvana* itself, viz. escape from *samsara*, escape from the cycle of birth-life-death-re-birth, but <u>not</u> an escape into nothingness, implies *something* transcendent.)

Nor is this notion of <u>an experience of</u> the transcendent peculiar to Buddhism. In virtually all of the major religions, there is a mystical tradition. A tradition that references people who (are alleged to) have had an experience of the transcendent, and practices that one can follow to put oneself in a position to have similar experiences. (In the three Abrahamic religions, such experiences are usually portrayed and thought of as being a gift from God and not as something you can actually achieve on your own, so to speak. In the Buddhist tradition I've just been speaking of, having such an experience <u>is</u> presented as being something you <u>can</u> achieve on your own. It may be hard to accomplish, in fact, very hard to accomplish, but it doesn't depend for its occurrence on any gift from a God.)

So, let's consider this possibility, the possibility of having an experience of the transcendent, with an eye to asking whether such an experience would justify thinking that something transcendent actually does exist.

As an example of such, let me go back briefly to the Buddhist tradition we've been considering, the Dzogchen tradition– the way of the Great Perfection. A brief description of the approach this tradition practices will give us some idea of how such an experience might be had and that, in turn, will reveal to us the implications and assumptions behind this approach more generally.

According to this tradition (and herewith an admittedly *very* brief and only partial description of it), one develops and refines the mind's abilities through a particular kind of meditation practice until you achieve the ability to focus on and attend to a given object with sustained, one-pointed attention. A state usually referred to as *samadhi* or *shamatha*. (These states are not quite the same, but the distinctions between them need not concern us here.) One is then in a position to engage in what is called insight meditation (*vipassana*). And applying your now-developed attentional abilities to the various contents of the mind one begins to 'see' and appreciate their dependent arising as well as their unbidden appearance and fading away. From there one focuses on the very 'space' of the mind itself. The 'space' in which such contents of the mind appear and disappear. And that leads to an awareness of something called the "substrate consciousness," the underlying level of consciousness that must be there for the individual mind to work at all. But this "substrate consciousness" is actually experienced, not merely inferred. And from there to the even more hidden or remote, "primordial consciousness"; that which must be there for there to be individual consciousnesses at all. And again, it is claimed that this is experienced and not simply inferred. And it is by means of this meditative process and sequence that one eventually attains insight into the true nature of reality; i.e. one has an experience of enlightenment or awakening.

And here (the interpretation of what enlightenment consists of), Buddhist traditions can really diverge, running the gamut from such enlightenment not involving anything transcendent to the position that it does. And even if one takes this second interpretation, that something transcendent is involved, there is a range of ways of identifying what that something might be. For example, here are some of the major contenders: the fundamental mind of clear light or the mind-vajra, *nirvana* (freedom from *samsara*), *sunyata* (emptiness), *dharmadhatu* (the absolute space of phenomena), *rigpa* (nondual awareness), jnana (primordial consciousness), and *dharmakaya* (the embodiment of truth). (The words in italics are transliterations of Sanskrit terms.)

I'll be taking the interpretation that something transcendent <u>is</u> being talked about and we can then ask whether an experience of anything transcendent is possible and if it is had, would that provide good evidence for the claim that something transcendent actually exists?

What would be examples of such experiences? There are numerous reports of experiences that would seem to imply the existence of something non-physical and of the non-physical being able to affect the physical. But I'll focus on just one kind of such experience. The one usually described as a "mystical" experience.

> As examples of other experiences that seem to involve either the existence of something non-physical or of something non-physical being able to affect the physical, there are: OBE's (out of body experiences), NDE's (near death experiences), PK (psycho kinesis) and TK (telekinesis), the placebo effect, telepathy and memory of past lives.
>
> Sometimes these have been shown to be simply hoaxes. Others have not been debunked, . . . yet. Still others have seemed impervious to debunking, e.g. some cases of the memory of past lives, and remain unexplained by any physical theory. Thus, at least in some cases, they *may be* evidence of something non-physical existing without depending on any physical substrate. I say *may*, because, e.g., an explanation of the phenomenon of memories of a past life involving "waves" of consciousness moving through space and persisting through time but originally produced by and therefore dependent upon brain activity, seems possible and has not, to my knowledge, ever been ruled out.

A mystical experience will here be taken as referring to any experience as a result of which, the person having the experience claims to have 'seen', i.e. to have come to *know*, some other reality (something very different from what we commonly understand of the world) and which they are absolutely convinced is revelatory (reveals what actually is so), and which is transcendent. In most religious traditions, this experience, this revelation, usually involves some kind of unity with an ultimate reality. In the Abrahamic traditions, it is a union with God, or Allah or Yahweh, but a union that does not deny or override in any way the distinction between creature and creator. These two remain distinct, but there is a closeness between them that, in some way, consumes or overrides the individuality of the creature.

In the Eastern traditions, that unity is much more one of identity. The revelation is that ultimately, the individual (and every individual) just is the same as, of the same 'stuff' as (?), the ultimate reality. *Tat Tvam Asi* (That thou art) and *Namasté* ('I honor that place in you where, when you're in yours and I'm in mine, there's only one of us') are classic expressions of this view in Hinduism.

Yet another way of expressing what one comes to know via such an experience is to say that the subject-object duality by which we understand and interact with the world in our normal, daily lives is, at some level and in some way, an illusion; that the only 'real' reality is something called non-dual awareness, e.g., and we are (of) that. Again, *Tat Tvam Asi*.

To return, then, to the question with which we began this little exploration. We asked whether <u>an experience</u> of the transcendent (or of transcendence?) would be good evidence for the claim that such exists? In order not to beg any questions, however, we really need to rephrase that question to read: would an experience *interpreted to be* of the transcendent (or of transcendence) be good evidence for the claim that such exists?

Interpreted to be **an experience of . . .**

49

Aye, and there's the rub, *interpreted to be*. Whether commonplace or unique, unremarkable or unforgettable, of no consequence or of great consequence, any experience we have is subject to interpretation. To simply have an experience is to become aware of *something*, and to know it or to be aware of it as a particular (kind of) "something" or even simply as this something, just_is to interpret the experience. Even if it is an experience you've never had before or an experience of something totally unfamiliar, you are immediately conscious of it as *something*, even if only as "something totally unfamiliar". At the least, it is interpreted as something that is *not* this or *not* that. Willy-nilly, it gets interpreted.

And this is important because it uncovers the assumptions that the RS must make in order to interpret any experience as a mystical experience. To identify an experience as mystical or transcendent, the RS must certainly think that something transcendent *could* exist. And beyond that, that it could interact with us (since 'it' is supposedly doing so in the very experience under consideration). And, finally, that one can come to know something in ways other than the ways of the strict scientific method (since the result of the experience is taken to be knowledge and the experience is <u>not</u>, usually, simultaneously available to an outside observer).

In other words, to claim that one can have (or that others have had) an experience of the transcendent, one has to make certain assumptions and those assumptions, it turns out, are the very opposite of the assumptions made by the SH, namely:

(1') **that something could exist which is neither physical nor dependent upon the physical for its existence;**

(2') **that the non-physical can interact with the physical;** and

(3') **that there are ways of coming to know that something is so other than the strict, classical scientific method.**

Assumptions Defended

The first assumption– that something transcendent can exist – is usually defended by an argument of the sort: whatever is not logically impossible is something that *can* exist. Thus, square circles cannot exist because they are logically impossible. But angels or demons could exist because they are not logically impossible.

The second assumption– that such a 'thing' or reality *could interact with* something physical– is somewhat trickier and more complex. It has two aspects to it: whether something non-physical *can cause some change* in the physical realm and on the other hand, whether we, humans, have the ability, the intellectual apparatus perhaps, to become aware of, to have a conscious experience of, something transcendent.

That first aspect or puzzle seems to derive from a primitive but very natural conception of any causation involving a physical entity, namely that the changed entity must be physically acted upon by the cause. Think of it as the billiard ball model of causation. Technically, this way of viewing causality is referred to as the principle of locality.

But quantum mechanics itself has called this principle into question with its demonstrations of quantum entanglement, where a change in one subatomic particle *instantaneously* causes a change in another, and far distant particle. And it does so much faster than even the speed of light. There simply could not be any physical interaction between the two particles by which the change in one causes the change in the other. Thus there are substantial grounds for thinking that actual physical interaction is not required to cause a change in something physical.

In addition, in this area of something non-physical being able to effect a change in the physical, there is the whole phenomenon of **"the placebo effect"**. This refers to the physical effect on a person's body and health that seemingly results from their *believing* something about a medication they've been given. There is considerable evidence that such an effect actually occurs. But there is no common consensus on how to explain it.

Nevertheless, it certainly *seems* that a belief (something non-physical) is having a physical affect.

But what about that second aspect? Are we (human beings) even capable of having a conscious experience of something transcendent, of the transcendent? People claim to have had such and claim that having such is attainable by others as well so long as they are willing to do the work, the preparation, for such an experience. (An argument from: people have had to therefore people can have. A classically legitimate argument form.)

They may all be lying, – delusion or conspiracy e.g., but it seems *very* unlikely that it would be the latter (conspiracy) since most of the people who have reported having such experiences were never in touch with one another. Perhaps the former (delusion) then? But the reports have been remarkably consistent among those claiming to have had the experience and this consistency has occurred over a significant period of history. And since these are the classic determinants of validity for the results of any scientific experiment, one would think that they should carry some weight here also in judging the reliability of these 'experiments' (experiences).

And finally, as to the assumption that we can come to know something other than by means of the scientific method. The argument is again one of arguing from what people have experienced to what people can experience. Everyday and constantly, we come to know things by means other than those of the scientific method. We know most of these 'things' through either introspection or intuition. And further, the process by which the knowledge occurs in either case is usually (always?) immediate. We don't take an inferential path to what is known, it just becomes apparent to us.

Thus, for example, we *know* what we are thinking at the present moment when we attend to it, and we know when and that we are experiencing fear, or awe or love. Sometimes we simply 'see' or understand a logical connection between propositions and for some fortunate and well trained mathematicians, they 'see' the cogency of a proof often before others who are equally well trained and sometimes years before anyone else ever 'sees' it. None of these instances of people coming to know something can be proven by or arrived at by the scientific method. But there is little doubt that they occur and are instances of knowledge.

Certainly none of these "defenses" *prove* the actual existence of something transcendent, but they are, at a minimum, strong evidence for the reasonableness and the plausibility of such claims.

And so we can return to the question we asked before (p. 44): would actually having an experience of the transcendent be good evidence for the claim that something transcendent exists? It certainly seems that it would be good evidence for the experiencer him or herself. The kind of evidence it would be hard for the experiencer herself to deny or doubt. Anymore, I imagine, than one could deny or doubt that you've had an experience of something that caused great fear or of something that caused wondrous elation in you.

But, you may doubt the identity of *the cause of* your fear – maybe you just thought you saw someone lurking in the shadows– but that you experienced fear, no? And that something caused that fear? No. I don't think you (or anyone having the experience) would doubt either. By the same token, you might misidentify the cause of your experience of the transcendent. Not, I think, that you had an experience of transcendence, (a seemingly transcendent experience?), but perhaps so as to *what* has caused you to have that experience.

And here is where "the rubber hits the road" so to speak. Is an experience of the (seemingly) transcendent revelatory or illusory? Is it revealing what actually is the case or is it only a mind state, which *appears to be* of something independent of that very mind state itself? How could one ever tell?

There is no sure fire way, but here is where "peer review" comes into play. I.e. having recourse to people both trained and experienced in the field to help you interpret what you have experienced. In science, examples of just this same recourse abound in the fields of astronomy and cellular biology and particle physics to cite but a few. To an untrained observer, what they see through the telescope or the microscope or in the cloud chamber is virtually unintelligible. That is, *the meaning* of what they see is virtually unintelligible. They need someone experienced in these disciplines, someone who has him or herself had the same experience and been able to compare notes with other researchers, both contemporary and historical, to be able to interpret the experience correctly.

So also in the 'field' of mystical experience. And the Eastern traditions, both Hinduism and Buddhism, are especially insistent on this. A virtually universal directive for new aspirants in either tradition is to find and have recourse to a teacher, a guru. And the main reason for this just is what we referred to above, viz. to be able with their help to correctly interpret what the aspirant is experiencing in their practice, especially in their meditation practice.

One final question: does having an experience of the transcendent require having adequate or appropriate (or at least approximate) words and concepts with which to comprehend the experience itself? Can anything be known or comprehended without concepts? And must you have such in order to even have the experience? Or is it that you would only need such in order to communicate the experience to others?

> This issue of whether or not we can come to know something without using concepts or categories to know it by is a contentious issue in Western epistemology. But it is clear that in the Buddhist tradition, they believe the answer to be: "yes, we can." The classical presentation of that position in Buddhism is shown in an episode of Buddha's life referred to as "The Flower Sermon."
>
> In this instance, so the story goes, Buddha came out to give a teaching to a gathering of his Sangha, and did nothing but stand there holding up a flower (no doubt, a lotus flower). The story has it that his disciples didn't quite know what to make of this 'sermon'. But eventually, one of them smiled, he got it, he knew what the Buddha was trying to say. And that was, that no matter what he might say about the flower, it would not <u>be</u> the flower, and yet <u>they could</u> come to 'know' the flower. That there was a way to come to know something without the use of concepts and categories and that using such in fact, failed to capture what the thing actually is or, at least, all that it is.

By talking with others and listening and reading, we already have an idea of what an experience of fear or awe or _____ is like and so can identify it when we have it. Or, someone who has had the same or a similar experience, a parent for example, names it for us.

While a mystical experience is certainly not as common as the experience of fear or love or elation, it is not unheard of. And language <u>has</u> been developed over the centuries to try to describe such experiences. Though admittedly, the less common the experience, the less precise and the more metaphorical the language to describe it will doubtless be.

55

So, it seems that one could have an experience of the transcendent, if such exists, and at least some would be in a position to correctly identify and even partially communicate their experience.

But what about those who have not had or not yet had the experience, would someone else claiming to have had such an experience be good evidence for them to think that something transcendent actually exists? And that, as was alluded to earlier, would depend on the credentials of those who claim to have had the experience. As in science, so too here. If the scientist in question is appropriately educated, trained and experienced and is respected by her peers, we are inclined to believe her testimony about something scientific which we have not ourselves experienced or perhaps experienced but not known how to interpret.

So too in this area of mystical experience. If the people making the claim to have had such an experience are appropriately trained, educated and experienced in the field, and are respected by their peers, we have some reason to take their testimony at face value, to assume they are accurately conveying what actually happened and are interpreting it correctly. And this, whether they are mystics in the Christian tradition or Arhats or Buddhas in the Eastern traditions.

To review: that initial assumption or axiom of the RS was that something transcendent *could* exist. But that, of course, didn't get us to: something transcendent *actually does* exist. We then looked at various ways such a claim might be supported and came down to what seemed like the most defensible way of doing so, viz. the fact that some people throughout the ages have claimed to have had an experience of the transcendent. And <u>if they are speaking accurately and honestly</u>, then that would be evidence that something transcendent *actually does* exist. Certainly it is taken as such evidence by the experiencer him or herself. It would be so for others only if those others had good reasons for thinking that such people were capable of interpreting and reporting their experience accurately.

We then looked at what reasons one might have for thinking that there were such people and looking at the historical record of such, their own training and efforts to be in the appropriate condition or situation for having such an experience and their lives after having the experience, and concluded that it might well be so. Further, we found enough comparable situations in life outside of this religious spiritual dimension (science, e.g. both in the rarefied experiences of various highly trained practitioners and in their recourse to peer review as a means of validating their experience) to grant that the same could well be so in the spiritual dimension as well. Thus, it is not unreasonable to think that some have had an experience of the transcendent.

Could it be communicated in such a way as to cause genuine understanding on the part of the listener? That someone has had such an experience could be communicated it seems to me. How much understanding of the experience might be thus generated is another matter altogether. How much understanding can one born blind ever have of the experience of seeing colors that a sighted person has? I suspect the answer is: not much. Or how much understanding can the average layman have of a scientist's description and explanation of what they have seen in some sophisticated experiment?

Similarly for one who has not had any experience of something transcendent. Any attempted expression of the experience on the part of the person who actually had the experience would have to be by way of approximation and metaphor (since being transcendent would entail being beyond conceptual capture). So the listener would be at least twice removed from the experience: they have not (yet) had it and so can't relate to it directly and any attempted description of the experience would be metaphorical. And thus, any second-hand understanding of an experience of the transcendent would indeed be as "through a glass, darkly".

****

What we have then, with these two sets of competing assumptions – those of the SH and those of the RS – are, in effect, two quite different explanatory systems. Two over-arching theories that are used to explain, understand and make sense of the totality of our human experience.

All this in just these three different axioms or assumptions? Not alone, of course, but they set the contours of each theory, their limits and structure if you will. And the really, really important thing about this is captured in something that Einstein is supposed to have said to Werner Heisenberg, viz.

> 'Remember Werner, what we see *is determined by* the theory we use to interpret our observations.' [Emph. mine]

In other words, the theory we use to interpret the data, the input, from our human experience actually precedes the experiences themselves. (In fact, the process is both interactive and iterative. Initially, when we're children, others (our parents, teachers, society) tell us how to interpret the input we receive. Later on, we modify our theories as they fit or don't fit the incoming data, always seeking for the best possible fit.) But the fact remains that in order to interpret *any* incoming data we have to have in place some theory that tells us *how* to interpret such data.

And so it is here. We have two quite different theories (sets of beliefs) which determine how we're going to interpret human experience(s). They set the limits on what will be taken as existing and of what can happen.

And again, as noted earlier, these two theories or sets of assumptions are not in conflict most of the time. Earlier we had said that the RS could and did accept much of what the SH held. It was only in one area where they significantly disagreed, viz. in the area of whether something transcendent could and did exist and could and did interact with the physical world.

And since both of these theories or sets of explanatory principles are based on foundational axioms or assumptions, there does not seem to be any way to rationally adjudicate between them. If you take <u>as a given</u> that only the physical (and what is dependent upon the physical) exists, then anyone who asserts the opposite will be seen as uttering a falsehood, and vice versa. More importantly, <u>if you take it as a given</u>, that only empirical data will be accepted as evidence for any claim about what exists, then there is no possibility of demonstrating that something nonphysical exists. You can't get behind or underneath a foundational principle because everything is interpreted in light of it, and all arguments to establish it, presume it.

It's not unlike Euclidean vs. non-Euclidean geometries, e.g. Riemannian geometry. If you take it <u>as a given</u> in your system of explanation that the shortest distance between two points is a straight line but the other theory asserts that the shortest distance between two points is a curved line, you're starting with two incompatible, basic, foundational axioms. They're not arrived at by inference from some more basic principles; they <u>are</u> the most basic ones *in that explanatory system*. They are the core, definitional assumptions or axioms on which you are basing your system.

Well then, what about comprehensiveness or completeness as a criterion for preferring one of these sets of assumptions over the other, one explanatory system over the other?

Generally speaking, any theory that is more comprehensive, which takes more of our experience into account, <u>is better</u> than one which does not and is to be preferred over one that explains less. But in this case, each theory 'explains' or has a place for everything in our experience. It's just that, at their limits, the 'place' for the transcendent in the one theory is in the category of "non existent" while in the other theory it's placed in the category of "existent". So that criterion will not help us choose between them in this instance. Assuming, of course, that the word 'exists' means the same in each instance. (Pace Clinton.)

Well then, what? Are we doomed to make no choice? Or, rather, no choice that can be rationally, logically established? Are we in a situation like Buridan's ass?

Perhaps not. Indeed, shouldn't the final, the ultimate proof, be "in the pudding" so to speak? "By their deeds shall you know them." How does either position influence how you live? And does this then provide a further reason (understood here more as a motive) for adopting one position rather than the other? Which position most promotes a life of hope and joy, a life of happiness or (as we'll see below) 'happiness' for you? Which helps you strive for and achieve that "more fully human" life we talked about in Ch. 2? And does this, then, constitute a reasonable and legitimate criterion for truth?

PART III

FROM COSMOLOGY TO COMPASSION

CHAPTER 6

<u>On Happiness</u>

We ended the last chapter with a question about the importance of those differing fundamental assumptions made by both the SH and the RS. We wondered if all that technical analysis was really important. Wasn't the more important thing: whether a person was happy and were they living a fulfilled and a fulfilling life? To answer this question, we'll need to inquire into what happiness is.

The literature on this subject is a vast one, as you can well imagine. So rather than trying to review it all here or survey the various arguments pro and con on the different ways of understanding the notion of 'happy', I am going to exercise an author's prerogative and simply accept what most commentators and thinkers who have dealt seriously with this subject seem to agree on, namely that for happiness to be truly satisfying, to have even a chance of lasting, or of leading to genuine contentment and satisfaction, it can't depend on acquiring stuff or things or even exotic and so-called peak experiences. (Anything that would range under the notion of hedonic. Consider, e.g., the oft referenced "drugs, sex and rock-n-roll".) And it can't depend on anything like that because that would make 'happiness' dependent on something outside of the individual's control and therefore undependable, inconstant and liable to be lost or taken from one. All of which, including just the fear of such loss, would then make you <u>un</u>happy.

No, for your life to be truly 'happy', for you to be fundamentally satisfied, content, at peace, fulfilled, – happy in that sense– it would have to come from somewhere inside you, from something that you alone control. (Indeed, might this even be the meaning of Luke 17:21, "the kingdom of God (or heaven) is within you"?) Something ultimately dependent, therefore, on your beliefs, on what you believe is valuable and good, and worth seeking. Something that you believe is worth achieving and therefore worth trying to achieve. Then, if you are engaged in that way, trying to fulfill that vision and realize that set of values, such desire and effort is not something that others or circumstances can take from you and the peace and contentment that is true 'happiness' can be yours.

> One problem with this view of things, but one which I won't deal with here, is how to account for someone believing that what is valuable and good, e.g., is something that actually harms other people or, more commonly, *some* other people. (Cf. e.g., the current battles in the middle east between the Sunni and the Shia Muslims, or between the Israelis and the Palestinians or that between ISIS and just about everyone else.) Couldn't they be expending their efforts to realize such goals and would their doing so cause them to be happy in the way we've just outlined? If happiness were taken to mean only a feeling state, then the answer would be "yes", it would be possible. But if happiness is referring to more than merely a feeling state, if it is rather taken to be referring primarily to an individual's way of being and whether that <u>way of being</u> was *in accord with* a greater reality, then "no", they couldn't be 'happy' on this view of things while trying to live a life that involved harming others. BUT, to support and defend this last claim involves getting into a whole discussion about what is true, whether anything in the realm of values (and morality) is *true* and why being "in accord with" whatever actually is the case would lead to happiness, and not being in accord would result in unhappiness, or incompleteness, in not being fulfilled. All of which would take us too far afield from the flow of this current train of thought.

So, being happy or, if you prefer, 'happy', depends in large part on what you think is valuable and good, and true. It depends on **value** and **meaning**. And the reason it depends on these is that what you value, what you think worthwhile, will determine what you want and want to achieve or realize in your life and therefore what you will seek and try to accomplish.

Well then, we might now ask: are there any differences, any significant differences, *here* between the SH and the RS? We saw before that there were significant differences between them in the area of their respective metaphysical and epistemological assumptions, in that part of their worldviews that reflected and were structured by those axiomatic assumptions. What about here, in the area of what's good, both non-moral and moral? In the area of what is truly valuable, what is beneficial to a human being and therefore worth seeking, and what is good in the sense of morally right, what *ought* to be sought and what *ought* to be done. Are there any significant differences here? More importantly, are there any differences that actually make a difference? Let's look first at **the non-moral realm** of what's considered good or valuable.

And what we find, I think, is that there is little or no disagreement between the SH and the RS on these things, on what is beneficial to a human being, on what is needed to live a fully human life and on what enhances doing so. Examples of such **non-moral goods** might be: beauty in all its various forms and dimensions; physical and mental health; the pleasures of the senses and the intellect; knowledge, affection (both giving and receiving), leisure and even . . . a good night's sleep. All of these are good and all of them play a part in living that "more fully human life". And all of these are typically thought good and considered part of what it is to have a full human life by both the SH and the RS. There doesn't seem to be any significant difference between them here.

If we think of such goods as comprising (at least in part) that "more fully human existence" which we talked about in Ch. 2, that conception of what it is to be a fully realized human being (or on the track to becoming such), then these are the goods that would go into

65

such a conception. (Moral goods, e.g. the attributes usually associated with character, (honesty, compassion, etc.), are also important to this conception of a "fully human life" but we'll deal with those separately in the next chapter.)

But the issue is different when we get to the area of **the moral good**, though even there, not initially so.

CHAPTER 7

<u>The Moral Realm – How we treat others, how one *ought* to live.</u>

If we understand the **"moral good"** to be referring to that area of human endeavor which deals primarily with how we do and *should* treat others, then at the initial level, the SH and the RS seem to be in full agreement. For example, both would agree that others, and <u>all</u> others, *should be treated* with dignity and respect.

I'll list some other areas of agreement below, but before I do, we should note that there is one more assumption at work here, one that these preferred ways of acting are themselves dependent upon for their status and acceptance.

To accept "treat <u>all</u> others with respect and dignity," or any similar dictum as one of those directives which best instantiates that "more fully human" way of being in the moral dimension, one must first start with the even more basic belief or assumption, namely that certain ways of behaving toward others <u>actually</u> are right and 'true'; i.e. that they actually do reflect or instantiate what *really is* the case both about people and about a "good" life – a "fully human" life– and that contrary ways of behaving are, in that same sense, not 'true'. In other words, **such directives presume that certain ways of behaving toward others actually do enable and promote what really is good for a person and contrary ways of behaving do not.**

All the more specific instances of beliefs about how one should behave, about what is the best way for someone to behave, (see below for some examples of such), are based on, depend upon, this ur-belief. It makes no sense to say that such-and-such a way of treating others is best for

67

them (and for society) *unless* there is such a thing as a "best way" (or at least a "better way") for someone or for society to be. In effect, that there is such a thing as a "more fully human" way of being.

Here, then, are some other examples of basic beliefs about how we should behave and which are agreed to by both the SH and the RS. We might think of these beliefs as second-order beliefs. They depend upon the truth of that ur-belief we just considered (small print above), but aside from that belief, these seem to be the most basic beliefs in this realm.

(1) It is better to be treated with dignity and respect than not to be.

At its most basic, this entails being allowed the freedom to determine (or not being interfered with by others from determining) one's own life-goals and the means of attaining those goals, *contingent always on the condition that* your pursuit of those goals does not thereby infringe on others' equal rights and freedoms.

(2) That from an impersonal (not subjectively driven) value standpoint (sometimes referred to, e.g., as from "God's viewpoint"), the good of any one person is <u>as good as</u> the good of any other person.

> In western, analytic philosophy this basis for morality is often referred to as "**the moral point of view**". The implication is that unless one is willing to take this point of view, one is not acting as a moral agent or in a truly moral fashion. You may be doing the "right" thing but you're not doing it for the right reasons or with the right motivation, you're doing it accidentally as it were, or perhaps even selfishly or manipulatively.

In Buddhist thought, this same notion– the good of any one person being as good as the good of any other– is what is referred to by the term translated as equanimity (*upeksha*). The base understanding of the term involves nondiscrimination or non-attachment to one's own good over that of others.

This can be a bit confusing to an English speaker since the first definition of 'equanimity' in English focuses more on the even-tempered-ness of a person, their calmness, and their disinclination to become agitated or excited. But in the four immeasurables of Buddhism, "equanimity" primarily involves this notion of nondiscrimination, of counting the good of all others equally. It compares closely to what in the West is called "the moral point of view".

One of the conclusions that can be drawn from such a position is that if it is good for me to be treated in a certain way, then it is good for all others to be treated in that same way. Where the "way" involved is described at an appropriately generic level, e.g. with kindness or with dignity and respect. And this, in turn, would lead to our being called upon to treat *all others* in that same way

(3) That what's "good" for any human being is whatever promotes his/her realization of a "fully human existence" (again!). As distinct, e.g., from "whatever he or she happens to desire at the moment".

(As an example of a position that adopts just this presumption, consider the Bill and Melinda Gates Foundation's professed mission of being dedicated to the proposition that: "Everyone Deserves the Chance for *a Healthy and Productive Life*.") [Emph. mine]

It is generally accepted that both the RS and the O/SH can and usually do get here, to these basic, 2nd order beliefs or moral directives. And it is these directives, and others like them that direct and express the multiple ways in which we help or try to help other people. This notion of *helping other people*, in turn, is exceedingly important in implementing that "spiritual guide" mentioned in the title of this book. And here is the critical linkage: trying to achieve what is really good in the moral realm involves helping other people achieve their more fully human existence.

I now want to look at *how* each (the SH and the RS) actually gets to these basic moral directives for that may give us some clues as to whether or not there are in fact any significant differences between them in this area.

How the religious spiritualist gets 'there'

At this stage of our reflections the 'there' we're speaking of in the heading of this sub-section is basically treating all others with both dignity and respect. And I will refer to it in this way through the remainder of this discussion. But the reader should keep in mind that doing so is shorthand for its fuller expression comprised of the three statements with which we concluded the previous section. And the question we're asking in this section is: how does the RS get to these beliefs and the actions that flow from them?

> It is important to note that this directive (treat all other people with dignity and respect) may well be considered by the religious believer to fall short of the maximum or the ideal of how they are to behave, and I will deal with that issue below. In the meanwhile we are looking at this directive about how we are to behave because it is commonly accepted by both the RS and the O/SH. And the question we are asking is: how does each "get there"? How do both the RS and the O/SH support or defend their commitment to this way of behaving?

One further note before we begin is that I'll be assuming throughout this discussion that we're talking about both the RS and the O/SH _at their best_. I.e. not just any "man on the street" who might self-identify as either an RS or an O/SH, but rather the informed and reflective proponent of each position.

A slightly expanded way of approaching this question would be to ask: **why do you think that <u>all</u> other people are deserving of being treated with dignity and respect?**

<u>Christianity</u>

For the Christian RS, I think the answer comes down to two basic reasons they usually give. (I'll deal with the Buddhist approach subsequently.)

The first reason that might be given is: because all are equally created by God, all are equally "a child of God". And as such, <u>all</u> are <u>equally deserving of being treated as</u> a child of God, as someone beloved by God. (Cf. e.g., the American Declaration of Independence, where all men [sic] being equally created by God is given as the reason for all being equal.) In that sense and to that degree, all are equal and all deserve the dignity and respect attendant upon such a state. This might be thought of as the metaphysical basis for the Christian of such a belief and the behavior that should follow from it.

The second reason that is often given to support this way of treating all other people is more concrete and historical in nature; it claims that we should treat all other people in this way because God has directed us to do so in the scriptures. As, e.g., in the directive to "love thy neighbor as thyself". And this approach might be bolstered by referencing the way Jesus is depicted as treating other people; even those usually despised and looked down upon in his society.

71

One problem with this second reason (for our purposes) is that it so easily leads into textual and historical analysis and criticism. E.g., did Christ *really* say that? And even if he did, what did "neighbor" mean to him and in his time and place? Etc. etc. In addition to the fact that I have no particular expertise in biblical exegesis and historical contextualizing, such discussions would take us too far afield from our focus in this chapter which is simply: what are the major reasons each side usually gives for believing that all other people should be treated with dignity and respect. And I think the two reasons just cited are the major reasons usually given by the Christian RS.

Buddhism:

For the Buddhist, things are quite different. There is no God in Buddhism, nor any instance of creation. So, everyone equally being a "child of God" simply doesn't apply. Instead, the Buddhist is more likely to approach the question from a combination of the metaphysical and the psychological. An example of this would be when they say that all equally desire happiness. (Where "happiness" does not refer to some kind of hedonic state of being, but is rather more in line with Aristotle's *eudaimonia*, a state of human flourishing not unlike that "more fully human existence" we spoke of before, and the peace and contentment that accompanies such and even simply striving for such.) In addition, all are subject to the same "obscurations and hindrances", the same impediments (ignorance/ delusion, craving and aversion) in the effort to achieve such a state.

And because all of us are the same in these regards, all of us deserve to be treated in a way that recognizes and respects this sameness; in ways that further our achieving such a goal and that recognize and take into account the obstacles we all face in trying to achieve it. These facts presumably lead to compassion and loving kindness, empathetic joy and equanimity– the four immeasurables of Buddhism.

But this basis does raise a question. How does one get from "all equally desire" to "all equally *deserve*" or *ought to be* treated in this way, minimally, with dignity and respect? The two concepts, of desiring and deserving, seem quite different nor is it obvious how one would entail the other.

The answer may lie partly (or even wholly) in the notion that being treated in such a way is not something *anyone* earns but is something that is due them based solely on what they are. In the Buddhist case, not children of God, but beings who all equally desire to be free of suffering. Though still, I must confess, *how* one goes from that feature of our humanity (assuming it is true) to our, and all, *deserving* to be treated in a certain way is hard to discern.

An alternative way of getting "there" which I have seen some Buddhist commentators take is to say that the ultimate reality in Buddhism, whether thought of as the absolute space of all phenomena (*dharmadatu*) or the primordial consciousness (*jñāna*), is "imbued with unbounded knowledge and compassion." In other words, they make compassion an integral component of the fundamental reality. And if that were so, then treating all others with compassion (which would certainly seem to include treating them with dignity and respect) would indeed be the right thing to do. It would be reflective of reality at its most fundamental, its deepest level.

In either case, the RS in the Buddhist tradition also seems to get there via a metaphysical claim. This is the way 'things' are, and because of that, all are to be treated with dignity and respect.

But whether it's Christianity or Buddhism, the important thing to note here is that in both cases, the grounds for treating all others with dignity and respect are based on an alleged fact about all people. In the case of Christianity, the metaphysical 'fact' of having been created by God and all equally being a child of God. In the case of Buddhism, the psychological-metaphysical fact of all desiring 'happiness' where 'happiness' means the kind of genuine human fulfillment that we've talked about in earlier chapters. Or the more purely metaphysical fact of the ultimate reality itself being imbued with compassion.

Note then, that in both religious cases, the obligation to treat others in a certain way does not depend on any <u>earned</u> <u>desert</u> on the part of the other. In both cases, it is based on what the person is or has, *simply as a result of* being created by God or of being a sentient being (a conscious entity). The grounding is metaphysical. This is a huge difference when compared with the grounding for such behaviors offered by the SH.

This metaphysical grounding also provides the rationale for including "all" humans in the prescriptive since all <u>are covered</u> by such a characterization.

In addition, such a metaphysical grounding also provides **a motivation** to behave in these ways, viz. the desire to act and to benefit from acting <u>in accordance with the way 'things' actually are</u>. Though the motivation could also be and more often, I suspect, actually is: because God (according to the Christian scriptures) or the authority of the Buddhist Suttas and commentaries, tells us to act in these ways.

In the Christian tradition, there is yet a third motivation for so acting, viz. because of a "personal relationship" with God. Thus, not so much out of simple obedience or, even less likely, the acceptance of some metaphysical reality, but out of 'friendship', out of being in a loved and loving relationship with God. (Cf. e.g., "accepting Jesus as your personal savior.")

And finally, there is a motivation that comes from an interesting and puzzling combination of the metaphysical and the scriptural, viz. Jesus' claim that "whatsoever you do to one of these, the least of my brethren, you do to me." Taken literally, this claim would seem to assert a unity, which, though highly motivational, is hard to reconcile with traditional Christian theology, which asserts an unbridgeable gap between creator and creature.

How the open or the secular humanist gets 'there'

And how does the O/SH get there? How do they arrive at treating others, and especially *all* others, with dignity and respect as the desired, the right way to act and behave?

Most often, the defense or argument for such a position is built upon a contractual framework. I.e., how would rational, self-concerned individuals agree to behave with other rational, equally self-concerned individuals where both have equal power?

John Rawls and Ronald Dworkin are examples of modern thinkers who have approached the issue in this contractual framework kind of way. And their conclusion, broadly stated, is that treating all others with dignity and respect <u>would be</u> arrived at, would be judged by all parties to the contract to be the way they agree to treat each other (and all others covered by the hypothetical negotiation and contract).

> This contractual basis is, of course, entirely hypothetical. It's not that people actually sit down together in the beginning of some social organization and hammer out an understanding that they're going to treat all other people with dignity and respect. For one thing, in real-life situations, the operative power arrangement among the participants is seldom equal all around. And for another, there are all the extant biases, tribal and family connections, history and culture which make it incredibly difficult to come to a rational, clear headed and fair

outcome. Instead, this contractual basis is an imagined one. Certain assumptions are made, certain provisos are put in place, and then it is asked what the outcome would be under those conditions from such a negotiation and assuming that everyone involved was acting rationally. John Rawls' *veil of ignorance* is a wonderful example of just such a hypothetical framework.

Can we be more specific in describing what it is to "treat all others with dignity and respect"? Presumably, and at a minimum, (and assuming a gradation of responses appropriate to the age and maturity of the person involved), these would include honoring others' ability to make life decisions for themselves and expecting their willingness to accept and either bear or enjoy the consequences of those decisions; to grant to all the freedom to make such decisions (always with the proviso that doing so does not thereby infringe on others' equal freedom); and to treat all others with the deference and courtesy owed such free and self-governing individuals. In short, to treat others in the manner and with the spirit that you would like to be treated.

Is treating others with dignity and respect, then, the same as the golden rule? Is it equivalent to what the RS arrived at? At a minimum, I would think so. But at the maximum, I think not. And more on that in a moment.

Some modern game theorists have argued that something less than the golden rule actually works out better in establishing a fair and well-functioning society. This "something less" has sometimes been labeled (with a nod to the rule labeled as "golden") as the "bronze" rule. But the bronze rule with modification. The bronze rule states that we should treat others as they treat us. And the important adjustment is: either start with a kind or a good or a compassionate act or occasionally respond with such an act even if the other party has just responded in an unkind or selfish fashion.

The game theorists' studies have shown that such behavior leads to the most satisfied community members and a social context perceived by those members as, generally, the most fair.

> Notice, however, that any "should" derived from this game theorist approach does not seem to be a moral should, but only a pragmatic one. It's not that one should treat others in this modified bronze rule way on pain of acting *immorally* if one doesn't, but rather that one *'should'* act in this way because doing so has the best chance of resulting in satisfaction among that society's members. The consequence of choosing to not act in this way is not so much acting immorally, but only acting unwisely, of not choosing the best means to a desired end.

There remains one last question to investigate as we consider how the O/SH gets to treating all others with dignity and respect. And that is: how do they get to the "all" in the "all others"? This is a critical component if we are to avoid tribalism or any other kind of favoritism and invidious discrimination in our treatment of others.

We saw previously that the RS got to the "all" on either metaphysical grounds or, often, on scriptural grounds. Based either on all are equally God's children or are equally created by God (again, cf. our own Declaration of Independence) or all are equally desirous of happiness and burdened with the same hindrances and obscurations. Alternatively, the "all" may be based on some directive found in the scriptures of the religion involved. (But here, as the reader can well imagine and perhaps has even experienced, both the textual and the contextual evidence can lead to vastly different interpretations of that "all".)

So then, how does the O/SH get to "all"? How do they get *to everyone* (i.e. no tribalism of any sort)?

One way of doing so is by setting the initial conditions for the hypothetical contractual negotiations referred to above in such a way that any of the usual or even possible grounds for discriminating me from you, or us from them, are excluded from the beginning. Rawls does this by putting all the participants to the negotiation behind a "veil of ignorance". Behind such a veil, no one knows beforehand what sex they will be, what color, what ethnic tradition, what citizenship, what religion, what their social status is, who their parents will be, etc., etc. Indeed, they do not even know what their own talents and abilities will be. Under such a condition, Rawls argued, the rational person would try to set up a society in such a way that any difference in treatment among the participants would only be allowed in situations where such a difference in treatment worked to the benefit of the least advantaged in that society. Everyone, he thought, would, if acting rationally, agree to this since one would not know whether it was him or her who were in that least advantaged position. Thus, not only is everyone involved in the negotiation (all rational beings), but also any grounds for later invidiously discriminating one person or one group from another are eliminated from the beginning.

Another way of getting to "all" is to set the conditions for an action or a behavior being a *moral* action or behavior at all. In other words, we have been speaking here of how we *should* (morally should) treat other people. So, if there is a condition which must be met before we can legitimately claim that any prescriptive or proscriptive rule or directive actually enshrines *a moral* obligation, then that condition would have to be met or be in place. And if, in addition, such a condition required the inclusion of all others, then for any action or behavior to be moral, it would have to be applied equally to all others. (Hence getting to the desired "all".)

This too, then, would be a way in which the O/SH might get to the "all" in our desired and obligatory ways of behaving, of treating all others with dignity and respect.

Thus even if we accept, at least for the moment, that the two positions– those of the RS and the SH– are *behaviorally equivalent* in their interpretation of what it is to "treat all others with dignity and respect", there is, as we have just seen, a difference in how that directive is grounded in either case.

In the case of the RS, the grounding is mainly metaphysical. In the case of the SH, the grounding is mainly procedural and analytic or reason-based. But whether this makes any significant difference we have yet to see.

> An interesting speculation that may throw some light on this question of whether the grounding, the basis, for such a directive is important, is: what are one's obligations, if any, in a case where you could flout the rules without any chance of ever being caught or known to have flouted the rules? Plato's *Ring of Gyges*, from his <u>The Republic</u>, is a classic effort to grapple with this possibility. Here, we might simply wonder if the differing bases for treating all others with dignity and respect (those of the RS and the O/SH) might lead to different answers to this puzzle.

Is treating all others with dignity and respect the end of the story?

This issue was raised earlier when we wondered if such a directive (even in its more complete expression) really captured what the RS meant by such phrases and directives as: "love your neighbor as yourself" and the even stronger "love one another as I have loved you ". And this last would seem to be echoed (actually, <u>pre</u>-figured) in the Mahayana Buddhist desire to become a Bodhisattva.

It is now time to revisit that question.

Is the game theorists' modified bronze rule then, the best that the SH can get to? Is it the rule, which, under the hypothetical contractual conditions imagined, the participants would actually come up with? Perhaps so.

But I believe there are even bigger reasons for thinking that the RS and the SH ultimately do not end up at the same place in their views of how one should treat all other people. To delineate those reasons and to explain the difference, I am going to adopt a particular way of labeling or referring to the two different ways of treating other people, viz. one as being at *the initial level* and the second as being at *the subsequent level*.

And is this 'there' the same?

The question we raised earlier in this chapter was whether or not the RS's approach to treating all other people (at its ideal) really was the same as the O/SH's approach (at its ideal). The question came up because it seemed, at first glance, that the two were not the same. And the issue came up at all because we were wondering whether the worldview one adopted– whether that of the O/SH or that of the RS– actually made any *practical* difference in one's life.

And what we found in our initial analysis was that these practical differences seemed to depend more on what we think is valuable and good or worth pursuing, and how we think we ought to behave. There seemed to be mostly agreement between the SH and the RS in the area of non-moral goods, at least when related to the notion of a "more fully human existence". And in the area of moral good, there was also a great deal of agreement on how we ought to behave, even though the grounds for arriving at such were quite different in the two cases. Now we are at the outer limits, so-to-speak, of such behavior (what we called the subsequent level) and are asking: are the SH and the RS the same at this level?

Again, I cannot emphasize enough that we're talking here of each side *at its best*, each side operating in accordance with its professed and stated rules or directives as those are understood and interpreted by most recognized experts in the field. Thus, for the RS, the multiple and various religious wars throughout history, the inquisitions, punishments for heresy, beheadings and other means of torture and killing that have been inflicted on opponents throughout history are seen as aberrations from their professed beliefs as those are understood by the theologians and the 'saints'. (And even here, sometimes, there are problems.)

And for the SH, the wars of aggression, the brutalities and atrocities done at the behest of greed, envy, lust and power, from slavery to the Holocaust and from Mao, Stalin or Pol Pot to Rwanda, are also seen as aberrations from the professed standards and ideals of the secular humanist.

So, the first difference between the O/SH and the RS was, as we've already seen, in their respective grounding for their directives. In the case of the RS, the grounding was largely metaphysical and then textually based obedience. In the case of the SH, the grounding was largely pragmatic and rational. Treat all others with dignity and respect because of something inherent in or about them, something which cannot, incidentally, be found empirically. Or, treat all others with dignity and respect because of enlightened pragmatism, because that works best in creating a workable human society.

But does it make any difference _why_ you're doing so? For the recipient of the action and at the initial level, perhaps not. Though perhaps it does even there. Would you rather be treated kindly and with respect because of some supposed inherent value that you possess or because it is assumed and been shown that if you are treated in this way, you are very likely to treat your inter-actor similarly? Or, do you even care _why_ you are being treated in a certain way as long as you <u>are</u> treated with dignity and respect? We'll come back to this, the motivation, shortly.

And wouldn't the SH claim that they also 'see' or believe that the other has *inherent value*? It's just not 'there' because of any relation to some God. Indeed, isn't the SH in virtually the same position as the Buddhist on this? No. Even though the Buddhist doesn't refer back to any creator God, or any God at all, they do refer to the individual's relationship to an ultimate reality that is not material as, finally, the ground of the individual's being and value.

More pertinently right now, however, it seemed that there was a subsequent level to which the RS aspired and sometimes went and to which the SH did not aspire or, at the least, aspiring to it was not a part of their worldview in this area.

This subsequent level is captured best, perhaps, in a saying or directive like: "Love one another *as I have loved you*" which, given the context of its utterance, implies or references **self-sacrifice** for the benefit of the other. This seems clearly to fall outside of the bronze rule and outside of simply treating others with dignity and respect.

And, as with Christianity, Buddhism also has a tradition that goes beyond simply treating all others with dignity and respect. In the Mahayana branch of Buddhism, there is something called "the spirit of Bodhicitta" and the goal of becoming a Bodhisattva. In the first, the desire is to achieve enlightenment or awakening *for the sake of all other sentient beings*. And in the case of the second, the desire to be a Bodhisattva, there is the intention and willingness to postpone one's own going into *final nirvana* and choosing to be reborn again *for the sake of* helping *all others* achieve enlightenment.

Is this difference, then, related in any important way to the differing bases on which the RS and the SH ground their directives on treating others? And if not, where does it come from? Purely from the textual references?

Grounding such a directive in the metaphysical worldview of the RS can be done, but it is somewhat tortuous.

In essence, it would involve (in the Buddhist tradition as well as in the Advaita Vedanta tradition of Hinduism) seeing the desired end-state of the individual as inextricably linked to that same end-state for all other conscious beings. So that the end-state would not be finally achieved until all were 'saved', until all were "in" that state. Then, sacrificing yourself for the good of the other would be noble, yes, but also supremely realistic and pragmatic. The final, final end has not been reached or achieved until all are enlightened. So the individual's achievement of nirvana is somehow and in some way, not quite complete by itself. The move within Buddhism from the Theravada tradition to the Mahayana tradition reflects this difference. And it was, presumably, motivated by the episode in the Buddha's life where, after he himself achieved enlightenment and was inclined to simply withdraw from interaction in the world, he is implored by the gods to share what he has learned with others who are also seeking enlightenment (and all are, whether they are aware of it or not).

A somewhat modified version of this same kind of explanation could also be put forward in Christianity ("the body of Christ" is a common way of referencing such a reality).

Though this might be stretching the similarity between Buddhism and Christianity in this regard beyond any easy recognition.

This subsequent way of acting is certainly more easily grounded in the scriptures of the various religions and in the lives of their founders, Buddha and Christ e.g.. And for now we'll leave it there.

However such a "subsequent way" of treating others is grounded, it is clear that there is a difference between the initial and the subsequent levels of treating other people in both intention and motivation as well as in action and in the presumed or believed context and consequences of so acting.

But having said that, it is also clear that both the OH and the SH are capable of and often do act in ways that are self-sacrificing for the good of the other. Whether it's falling on a hand grenade to protect your buddies or sacrificing much of your personal life to take care of an elderly parent or sacrificing your own safety and financial position to aid others in need (e.g. the volunteers in Doctors Without Borders), the SH also, often, engages in self-sacrifice for the well-being of others. Doing so is not peculiar or restricted to the RS.

For the RS, the intention and motivation behind treating others **at the subsequent level** is to respond to them and reflect in one's response to them, what they are, supposedly, at their core. Textually, in Christianity, this is captured in the saying: "Whatsoever you do to one of these, the least of my brethren, you do to me." In Hinduism, by _namasté_ ('I honor that place in you where, when you're in yours and I'm in mine, there's only one of us'). And in Buddhism by the unitary nature of the primordial consciousness or, in Hinduism's Advaita Vedanta, of the non-dual awareness.

For the SH, it's not so clear what the motivation might be. Perhaps it is simply a conviction that treating others as you _would like to be_ treated is indeed an ideal worth striving for regardless of what the game theorists say. But whatever the motivation, it is clear that the SH can and equally often does act in a self-sacrificing way.

> This is a puzzling issue: what could the motivation be for a SH to engage in self-sacrificing behavior? It would seem, on some accounting, to be an inconsistency on their part, a position that conflicts with their stated or unstated

conviction that this life is all there is. For example, one could argue that if this life is all there is, then any chance the person has to either experience or promote truth, beauty and goodness is lost if their life is lost. So logically, it would seem, there would be nothing more important to the individual than preserving his/her life. And if there were nothing more important to a person than preserving his life, then self-sacrifice, at least at that level, would be irrational. It is to hold something else as more valuable than what you are committed to as being most valuable (the preservation of your own life). And isn't that to be inconsistent and self-contradictory? All of which would seem to argue for not sacrificing your life, whether literally or effectively. And yet, as I noted in the main text, the SH often does so.

Earlier secular humanists such as Schopenhauer, Nietzsche, Camus, and Sartre perhaps perceived just such a dilemma which caused them to shy away from an outright nihilism and counsel instead, as in Camus' case, courage in the face of meaninglessness as the more humane and human response.

At the initial level of treating others, there did not seem to be much or any significant difference between the RS and the SH in how they would behave and what they would perceive their obligations to be. Though **the intentions and motivations** behind those actions might be different, the behaviors prescribed seemed to be pretty much the same.

But **the context and consequences** of so acting *are believed to be* quite different in each case. For the SH, the context is practical, legal, and moral. And the consequences are here-and-now, into the historical future and wholly within time and space. Not so for the RS. For the RS, the context is metaphysical and transcendent (the only way in which such claims of identity ["whatsoever you do to one of

85

these . . . "], e.g., can make any sense) and some of the consequences are, it is believed, eternal – outside of time and space.

But in both cases, it is clear that **helping others** and more expansively, helping others to achieve that "more fully human" existence, is seen as the main way (the only way?) of incorporating the moral good into our lives on our way to 'happiness'. So again we can ask whether the differences between the O/SH and the RS in this area really make any difference?

If you mean do they make any difference in the physical action as observed by a bystander or even, perhaps, by the recipient him or herself, perhaps not. Indeed, almost certainly not in many cases.

But do they make a difference to the actor and to the recipient of the action in ways that may not be observable from the outside? If intentions and motivation affect the quality of an action (again, consider Plato's story of The Ring of Gyges), and if the context and (believed) consequences can affect its manner of expression, then these differences clearly can make a difference.

So, yes. These differences in intention and motivation, in (believed) context and consequences do make a difference, and even a difference that could be empirically measured in some cases. But whether measurable or not, a difference at the conscious and felt level certainly by the actor and perhaps also by the recipient.

And these differences are, ultimately, dependent upon one's worldview, on those fundamental assumptions and axioms that form the basis for the superstructure of our beliefs and judgments about the world and our place in it. But they are even more proximately dependent upon a couple of further assumptions that each side makes. And for that we turn to the next chapter.

CHAPTER 8

<u>Assumptions in the Realm of Meaning and Value</u>

So, we're trying to figure out if those earlier metaphysical and epistemological assumptions made by both the SH and the RS (Ch.'s 4 & 5) actually make any difference when it comes to how people live their lives and whether they're happy. And we decided that these two issues seemed more dependent upon what people considered valuable and worthwhile, what they considered good (both non-moral and moral) and worth seeking. (Ch.'s 6 &7) In this chapter we're now going to consider the other component that seems critical in determining what makes people happy (or 'happy') and whether their lives are fulfilled and fulfilling, viz. the whole notion of meaning.

"Does life have any meaning?" "Is there any point to it all?" These short questions can pack a lot of wallop. They are often uttered and even more often, I suspect, felt or uttered silently by most of us at some point(s) in our lives. They are both a plea for insight into and an understanding of our place in the universe and a worry that the answer the universe will give to each question is "no".

Not, of course, simply "no", full stop. But "no" in the sense that there is no meaning, no significance to our lives, *beyond* whatever meaning we invest them with *and beyond* whatever impact they happen to have on the people we encounter both now and, by reputation or influence or product, for some time into the future. Rather, the "no" means there is no *transcendent* meaning to our lives; no meaning beyond and other than what can be seen and heard and documented as occurring in our world of space and time.

And "is there any point to it all?" usually wonders, similarly, whether everything that happens and everything that we (and all others) do, fits into some purposeful whole? Does the world, the universe, do our own actions play a role in completing some whole? And not a whole that is simply a notional collection of everything that has ever happened, but a whole that comprises a vision of what is good and one that is lasting.

It will turn out, not surprisingly, that the SH and the RS here also have quite different takes on these questions. Here also, we'll find, they each subscribe to quite different fundamental assumptions in answering these queries. And as we examine their respective answers and assumptions we'll also encounter one of the most common and stronger challenges to the RS's position, viz. the question posed by the SH to the RS: "but aren't you just engaging in wishful thinking?" A consideration of these three, then, will form the content of this chapter.

Do our lives and does what we do have any meaning beyond what is visible, what can be empirically verified, in the here and now or in the future? Our actions certainly have a formative effect on our characters (and vice versa), but do our characters have any impact on us beyond the grave? (Assumes, of course, that there is something beyond the grave for the individual. I'm not assuming any answer to that here but only pointing out the usual import of that question.)

Another way of approaching this same question (though not a way that is immediately obvious) is to ask whether intentions count. Do the unseen, non-empirically verifiable, intentions that guide most of our actions count for anything? (This issue was raised before when we referenced Plato's story about the Ring of Gyges.) And again, the real issue becomes: do they count for anything beyond the grave, since they clearly "count for something" here and now, viz. in the formation of one's character and that, it could be argued is empirically testable.

The "beyond the grave" context in this regard is often contained in the question: is character destiny?

Does life have any meaning?

Given the current context for this question (see above), it can be rephrased as: does it make any difference what I do? Will how we act and how we live make any difference in the final outcome? If, in the end, it's all just dust or energy dissipated to such an extent that the universe is nothing but a frozen tableau of planets and burnt out stars, then it would seem that *ultimately* it doesn't make any difference what I do. If the end is the same no matter what I or anyone else does, then whatever we do hasn't made any difference. At least it hasn't made any *ultimate* or final difference, either for me (or you) or the universe.

Proximately, of course, what we do does make a difference. It makes a difference to the people affected by our actions both here and now and into the (at least) foreseeable future. And it makes a difference to the degree that our actions cause either harm or well-being. But this proximate only meaning of our lives is not enough for some people. And here is one more place where the SH and the RS part company. For the SH, that proximate- only meaning is enough, because it's the only reality. And for the RS, such proximate-only meaning is not enough. To them it does not give sufficient weight to our intentional actions, to the way(s) we choose to live our lives. If this "vale of tears" is seen as essentially a 'vale of soul-making', then there must be some consequence, some ultimate and lasting consequence for the result of that soul-making and for the efforts that go into it. There "must be", the RS avers, if life is to have any meaning.

This whole difference of viewpoint can be summarized in the following question:

Is the universe lawful in the moral realm as it is in the physical realm?

Is it the case that for all of our intentional actions, there is a similar and proportional consequence for the actor, either now or in the future? (Note the very intentional similarity in this phrasing to that of Newton's third law of motion: for every action there is an equal and opposite reaction. A similarity meant to emphasize the lawful nature of such a regime independent of any particular act by, e.g., an all-seeing judge or God.)

For a fuller analysis and discussion of this question, see the author's earlier work: <u>Some Thoughts On The Big Questions</u>, pp. 20 - 42.

The SH answers this question in the negative. There *may* be such similar and even proportional consequences for the actions we intentionally undertake, but there is certainly no guarantee of such, there is nothing lawful about it. And even more certainly, there is no future beyond the grave in which they might occur if they don't occur in the here and now. The RS answers this question in the affirmative. There are such consequences and it may often be the case that they occur only in some future beyond this life.

But neither answer can be proven. Both are equally *beliefs* and equally assumptions on which fuller and more expansive worldviews are built. So, the final assumptions we are dealing with are in answer to the question: is there any point to it all? And those assumptions are: either affirmative or negative stances on the propositions that

there is some point to it all and

the universe is lawful in the moral realm as it is in the physical realm.

Where, again, the driving question is taken to mean: is there some end result for everything that exists which somehow realizes or comprises a whole that is both good and lasting and in which every component plays a role in achieving that end state, and a role which somehow contributes to the completeness of that end state? Teilhard de Chardin's Omega Point would be an example of such a belief from a Christian perspective. Buddhism, to my knowledge, does not have a specific name for such an end state, but they would certainly say that there is some point to it all, viz. that all sentient beings achieve final nirvana.

Another way of thinking of this question is to liken it to the physicists' *theory of everything* or their ToE. Physicists (at least many such) have for some time now believed that there is a theory covering the physical universe which will allow them to explain how all the four fundamental forces (gravity, the strong and weak nuclear forces and electromagnetism) fit together. Right now, the two major theories in physics, General Relativity and Quantum Field Theory, cannot individually account for everything that exists in the physical world. One does a good job of explaining the macro world of planets and stars, cars and buildings, dogs and people. The other works well at the micro level of atomic and subatomic particles. But they cannot be reconciled, as currently understood they are incompatible. Nevertheless, most physicists believe that there is some theory, dubbed the Theory of Everything or ToE, which will be able to unify all of these fundamental forces. They are convinced that it does all fit together in a unified and coherent whole. And, I suspect, most secular humanists who are even passingly familiar with this field, and care, would agree with such physicists. But this too is *a belief* and a hope. There is no guarantee that such a ToE exists. It just seems to be required by the ur-belief that rational sense can be made of the world. That its obvious lawfulness in many areas *must be* extendable to all areas; that the very conviction that drives any of the individual sciences must be true of the universe as a whole.

The religious spiritualist would say that their view on there being some point to it all is similar. It's also a kind of ToE, but one which includes not just the material world but also the subjective world of human thought, beliefs, intentions and actions, a world of mind and consciousness and soul, a world of good and evil where these are viewed as more than just conventional definitions. And their conviction is equally a belief and a hope.

But, it might be said, "that's just wishful thinking."

And this brings us to one of the most common responses of the SH to both of the beliefs we've just looked at, viz. 'you (the RS) are indulging in wishful thinking; time to grow up and leave the fantasies and hopes of childhood behind, face facts and live in the real world.'

Typically, this charge and advice comes on the heels of the RS speaking of heaven or some reward for living a good life or for some form of ultimate justice, either of which requires some kind of continued existence for the self beyond the grave. This, it is alleged, is just silly or jejune or immature thinking on the part of the RS. 'There is no God 'in the sky' or any afterlife in which all "boo-boos" will be kissed and made better. Get over it.'

The first thing to note about this charge is that it often (usually?) leaves out the justice part of the RS's vision or belief system. It's not the case, according to the RS's view of things, that everything will be better in the future, full stop. Not at all. In the Abrahamic religious traditions, there is also hell to contend with. And in the Eastern religions, there is karma and re-incarnation or rebirth. The underlying belief for both traditions is rather something like: character <u>is</u> destiny. The belief that we can, by how we live, affect what ultimately happens to us; that good or moral actions and behavior will have good consequences for the actor, and that bad or immoral actions will have negative consequences for the actor.

Note that the SH could actually agree with the RS up to this point. Good actions <u>will</u> have good consequences for the actor and evil actions will have bad consequences for the actor. Where they differ is in the time frame involved for such consequences and in the belief that there is (or will be) *proportionality* between the action and the consequences for the actor. For the RS, great or horrendously evil actions will have great consequences for the actor (hell, e.g., or maybe being reborn as a slug or having to go through many, many rebirths). And great or persistently good actions will have proportionately good consequences for the actor. The SH bails at this point because it is so obvious to anyone that such proportionality often (usually?) <u>does not occur</u> <u>in this life</u>. For the RS to claim it, they <u>must</u> depend on there being some form of afterlife which the SH rejects.

In any case, the RS's vision is hardly Pollyannaish. Indeed, it could be argued that it is harsher than the SH's, since, putting it in the vernacular, you don't get away with anything on their view of things (vs., for the SH, if you die before justice is done, you've escaped free-of-charge, so to speak).

But it is quite instructive to look at the explicit or implicit arguments behind the SH's charge of wishful thinking. What is the actual argument that the SH is making in this challenge to the RS? It appears to be something like:

1) Because you (the RS) would like that to be the case (either or both of the two fundamental assumptions of the RS discussed earlier in this chapter), you're claiming that <u>it is</u> or <u>they are</u> the case.

2) But merely wanting or wishing that something be so is no grounds for claiming that it actually is so.

3) Therefore, you have absolutely no grounds for thinking that either of those fundamental assumptions is actually true.

In response to 1) the RS would say: 'No, no. I would like it to be so, but that's not the reason I believe it is so. It's an "and". I would like it to be so and I believe that it is so.'

And if pressed to actually state his reason(s) for thinking it is so, the RS might say something like this: 'if the world, the universe, everything that exists, is structured in this way (in accordance with those two earlier assumptions), then it all fits into a whole. It all comes together to make sense. It's much like the physicist's belief that there is a ToE, which all the forces of nature and everything that flows from and is affected by them do fit into a unified, coherent whole. And as I see it, the human world of actions and intentions, goals and impulses, likes and dislikes, is also something that exists and is also something that cries out for a place in that whole. These two assumptions define the whole in which this world of human intentional action finds its place.'

And note that the focus here is not on the viability of such a reason offered by the RS, rather it's on the point that he has a reason that is *quite other than* that he simply wishes it were so. He likens his reason to that which the physicist might use to support his view that there is a ToE, viz. that things make sense if there is a place for everything, if it all comprises a unified and coherent whole, and one that is continuous with the coherent but incomplete whole we have discovered or described so far.

A second argument the RS might use to counter this charge by the SH would be that this wishing for some ultimate justice and for our intentions and motivations to be taken into account in any final outcome, are not grounds for thinking that such exists in the sense that they constitute premises of an argument which concludes to such a state. But, they may be something like indicators that such a state exists. Here the thinking would be more along the lines of St. Augustine's: "Thou has made us for thyself O Lord, and our hearts are restless 'til they rest in Thee." I.e., the virtual universality of this strong desire or wish for a universe in which our actions and intentions actually do have an effect on us that is both similar and proportional to their own character is seen as an indicator of something that actually fulfills that desire. Something like a universe that is lawful in the moral realm.

But perhaps the strongest counter to this charge of wishful thinking is to simply lay out what seems implied by the argument. Suppose it is wishful thinking *in the sense that* most people <u>would like it to be the case</u>. (Though our earlier point of: you don't get away with anything on this view of things might well be a point against this claim of "most people would like . . .") Can one reasonably conclude that therefore <u>it</u> <u>is not</u> the case? You could not. At least, not without assuming a missing premise (MP) something like:

1a) Most people would like to believe that there is some point to it all or that the universe is lawful in the moral realm.

MP) If X is something that most people would like to believe is true,
then X <u>is not</u> true.

3a) Therefore, it is not true that there is some point to it all or that the universe is lawful in the moral realm.

But I can see absolutely no reason for thinking such a premise, the (MP), to be true.

So, contrary to the charge of wishful thinking, the merely wishing it, <u>is not</u> the reason or grounds for the RS believing it to be so and even if it were, that alone would not be any grounds for thinking that it is <u>not true</u>.

CHAPTER 9

The Complete Worldviews . . .
and Their Assumptions

So, each of the O/SH and the RS holds a worldview, a theory or an explanatory framework for understanding and comprehending what is the case, for what is true about the world or universe, our lives, and how they fit (or don't) into the universe.

And each explanatory framework has certain assumptions or axioms that it takes as fundamental and given, not able or needing to be defended or proven. Here's a listing, with brief commentary, of the complete set in each case.

FOR THE SECULAR HUMANIST VIEW, they are:

> **Only the physical or what is caused by the physical exists**.
> The matter-energy dyad – in all its various manifestations– exhausts what can be and what actually is.
> (For an extended commentary on 'matter' and its various meanings, cf. Ch.4.)
>
> **There is no way for anything non-physical to interact with something physical or vice versa.**
>
> **The only way to come to really *know* anything is by way of the scientific method.**

(The first two of these basic positions are metaphysical in nature; the last is epistemological in nature.)

And, as one might expect, <u>THE RELIGIOUS SPIRITUAL POSITION</u> had similar but opposite basic assumptions, to wit:

> **That something transcendent (something neither physical nor dependent upon the physical for its existence) can and does exist.**
>
> **That something non-physical *can* and does interact with something physical and vice versa.** And
>
> **That there are ways of coming to *know* 'things'– to know what is so – other than (in addition to) the strict scientific method.** (And among these "other ways" is subjective experience itself.)

Usually these metaphysical and epistemological assumptions or axioms are treated as argument-stoppers rather than argued for themselves.

Indeed, it is not clear that they <u>can</u> be argued for without begging the question (or defining your way to the desired conclusion). E.g. concerning the question of whether something non-physical and not dependent upon the physical for its existence actually does exist. The answer will obviously depend on what you're willing to accept as evidence for the answer. And usually (always?), the SH (the materialist) will not accept anything other than something physical as evidence. Case closed. Or, argument 'won' by default, by <u>apriori</u> restricting the range of 'facts' that will be accepted as evidence. But any restriction that assumes what is to be proved, simply begs the question.

And similarly so with the RS. When attempting to answer this same question, he or she usually starts with: it *could be so* (something non-physical and not dependent upon the physical for its existence *could* exist based on there being no logical contradiction in such a state of affairs). And then, she appeals to experiences, (her own or others') that involve 'things' that are pretty clearly not physical (initially, e.g., ideas, feelings, hopes, etc.) _plus the claim that they are not dependent upon the physical for their existence_. (Cf. the causation vs. correlation discussion had earlier in Ch. 5.) Again, case closed. In this case, position 'won' by an interpretation that itself just begs the question.

The assumptions we've just reviewed all fell into the categories of metaphysics and epistemology. But what was and is most intriguing about them is their centrality, indeed, their virtual universal commonality for anyone holding the respective worldviews we've been considering. Only the first of these axiomatic-like propositions is absolutely required of anyone holding the respective worldview, but the remaining two propositions seem to always accompany the first in each case. And there doesn't seem to be any way of establishing them that doesn't presume them. They appear to be foundational axioms in their respective systems of explanation. This is really quite arresting, and sobering. How many secular humanists or religious spiritualists have ever stopped to consider that if they believe as they profess to, then they _must_ be holding one or the other of these foundational beliefs?

But these assumptions and axioms 'live' in a pretty rarefied atmosphere that can sometimes seem far distant from our daily lives and concerns. Concerns about how one ought to live and how to be happy. So we shifted gears, so-to-speak, and began to look at these latter questions. (Ch's 6 & 7) And after settling on a widely acknowledged and proposed meaning for genuine 'happiness', we then focused on the question of how one ought to live. Both in the sense of how to obtain that happiness and in the sense of how one ought to live a moral life. And this led us through a review of how the RS and the SH each got to their respective prescriptions. But most importantly, it got us to the realization that their respective prescriptions were not entirely the same. They agreed on much and were virtually the same at a basic level (at what we later called the initial level), but they eventually diverged at what we called the subsequent level. And this divergence was found to once again reflect a pivotal divergence in certain underlying assumptions on each side.

There are also opposing assumptions or axioms in the realm of meaning and value.

In these cases also, the axioms involved seem to be an essential component of the materialist's or the religious spiritualist's worldview. They are not necessary for either worldview, but as usually construed and affirmed, they are always present.

> I say "as *usually* construed and affirmed" because the deist position would seem to be an instance of an RS who does not hold either of the meaning and value assumptions we've been considering.

For the RS, the fundamental assumptions or beliefs in this area are:

There is some point to it all.

The universe exists; we exist, for a reason, to achieve a certain end (and not simply the end of: however it all *happens* to end). There is some reason that anything exists and for everything that exists. Some reason *why* they exist. Everything, including us, somehow plays a role in a final outcome. A final outcome that is both good and lasting, though not necessarily predetermined either in whole or in its particulars. (Note: this position looks like it either presumes or is positing a creator, but it need do neither.) This sense of things is well conveyed by Vaclav Havel when he says:

> "Hope is definitely not the same thing as optimism. It is not the conviction that something will turn out well, but the certainty that something makes sense, regardless of how it turns out."

And the second fundamental assumption of the RS

The universe is lawful in the moral realm as it is in the physical realm.

And that lawfulness governs the history, development and outcome of one's intentional actions as much as the laws of physics govern the workings of the physical world. Character <u>is</u> destiny. And again, Havel captures it well when citing Dostoevsky's spiritual dictum that all are responsible for all, he refers to that

> "'higher' responsibility, which grows out of a conscious or subconscious certainty that our death ends nothing, because everything is forever being recorded and evaluated somewhere else, somewhere 'above us,' in … an integral aspect of the secret order of the cosmos, of nature, and of life, which believers call God and to whose judgment everything is liable."

And for the SH,

<u>There is no point</u> to it all.

There is no point to it all other than: survive while you're here, for as long as you can and want to (and no doubt, as well as you can). Your life does not play any role in the existence or structure of a final outcome other than as a purely adventitious and historical component. Indeed, the only "final outcome" there is, is either the heat death of the universe or, possibly, some perpetual cycle of expansion, contraction, big bang, expansion and contraction of the universe, <u>ad infinitum</u>. And

The universe <u>is not</u> lawful in the moral realm.

Indeed, the SH would question whether any meaning can be given to such a claim at all. But at the least they would say that morality and moral rules/laws are purely a human creation and do not reflect any 'deeper' reality; that any notion of there being inescapable, proportionate and anodyne consequences for our actions in the moral realm is simply immature and wishful thinking.

As noted earlier, these differences in theory or in explanatory framework can play an enormous role in the attitudes and spirit with which the opposing adherents approach their lives.

In the case of the RS, they often approach their lives with a spirit of motivation, trust and hope, perseverance and joy. Which is not to say that they are Pollyannas, but only that they have the conviction that, in the end, the final outcome both for themselves and for the universe, will be good.

But this is not to say that the SH cannot also approach life with a sense of motivation and hope, perseverance and joy. It's just that when they do, the time frame in which these emotions and convictions operate is much shorter and, perhaps, more subject to alteration by life's circumstances. And of course, there is no ultimate trust, no trust other than the trust that one places in one's self and one's ability to affect the proximate outcome in any situation, and sometimes, perhaps, also a trust in the basic goodness and love of others.

So what is one to do? Is there no way of deciding between these worldviews, these explanatory frameworks? No, non-question-begging way?

It seems that the secular humanist always has the fall back position of: it (anything that we have experienced) either is physical or is dependent upon something physical for its existence. Though, in some instances, they admit, we don't yet know *how* it is so dependent (for example, *how* consciousness derives from brain activity), we don't yet know the mechanics of it so-to-speak. It is, they claim, nevertheless clear that *it is* <u>so</u> <u>dependent</u>.

And the religious spiritualist can always fall back to: 'well, there's nothing logically impossible about something transcendent existing, (= it *could* be so), and there are enough instances, throughout history and across varying traditions, of people who claim to have experienced something transcendent, to support the claim that *it is so*.'

The secular humanist, the materialist, as we saw, runs the danger of confusing a heuristic for a metaphysical truth. She runs the risk of extrapolating from a method of inquiry and proof (the methods of empirical science) to the claim that only those 'things' susceptible of such inquiry and proof actually exist.

The religious spiritualist runs the risk of wishful thinking.

And both the secular humanist and the religious spiritualist are equally dependent, in how they view or understand and explain the world, upon interpretative frameworks that are prior to any experience to-be-interpreted, but interpretive frameworks that are not simultaneously compatible. Both views, both explanatory frameworks, can be supported by the facts *because they are actually prior to and determinative of* the facts, of what's presented to us in our experience. Indeed, they actually determine what is to count as a "fact." (Refer back to our earlier discussion of Einstein's caution to Werner Heisenberg: 'Remember Werner, what we see is determined by the theory we use to interpret our observations.' (Ch. 5)

So where does that leave us? Trapped in an irresolvable dilemma? "There is nothing beyond the physical and whatever is caused by the physical" and "no, something does exist which is neither physical nor dependent upon the physical for its existence." And is there any need to choose between them?

In short, yes, there is a "need". And the "need" is driven by logic. These two explanatory systems are not compatible. I.e., IF they are each asserting that their worldview encompasses **all that exists**, then, as we've seen, there comes a time when they don't agree (viz. the fundamental assumptions), and since these fundamental assumptions are contradictory, no contrasting pair of them can both be true (or false), if one is true, the other must be false and vice versa.

> This issue of the compatibility of the scientific and religious worldviews has long been and is still much debated. A relatively recent example, and one often referred to, of an attempt to resolve any apparent conflict is Stephen J. Gould's "non-overlapping magisteria". According to Gould, the two worldviews are not ultimately in conflict because they are referring to two different realms of being. The scientific realm is that of empirical reality, matter and whatever is susceptible to detection by our senses or their instrumental extensions. Whereas the religious worldview, on Gould's account, is dealing with the spiritual realm, where that term is taken as referring to the transcendent as we have characterized it in this book. And if these two realms are incommensurable, talking about two entirely different realities, so realities that cannot be contrasted and compared, then both worldviews could be correct, but only in their own distinct and non-overlapping worlds.

> This is tempting. But I think it ultimately fails (the position I've taken above in the main text). And I think it fails because of that phrase, "IF they are each asserting that their worldview encompasses <u>all that exists</u>." And each side <u>is</u>, usually, so asserting. Their worldviews are meant to be all-inclusive. Neither side thinks they are only accounting for some of reality.

> But what about my earlier claim that the RS can and does accept the methods and findings of science? Doesn't that

imply two different realms, as it were? And the answer is in part, yes, but finally, no. *How* something exists may be different, e.g. as a material entity susceptible to scientific investigation or as a spiritual entity not subject to scientific (empirical) investigation. But both <u>do</u> *exist*. (Where *exist* means something like: are able to be known, have certain attributes, and are able to cause change.) And if both sides in this dispute claim to be covering <u>everything</u> that *exists* by their respective worldviews, then no, they are not finally compatible.

Put another way, the RS can accept any scientific claims made by the SH because they are in agreement that the claim made is about empirical reality. It's only when, and if, the scientist goes on to make the metaphysical claim: "and that's all that exists" that the RS parts company with her. At that point, the two worldviews become incompatible.

'Well, that's kind of uncomfortable. And awfully absolutist wouldn't you say? I mean, where's your tolerance? Indeed, where's your humility? You think you know it all?'

Of course not. I'm not saying <u>which</u> view one has to hold or which view is the right worldview. I'm only pointing out that you cannot, rationally, hold both simultaneously. If one is true, the other must be false. If the box is empty, it can't also and at the same time be full. A choice must be made. And what we're going to look at in chapter 11 are some of the reasons one might have for choosing one worldview over the other.

But before we do, there is one final subject to consider. It has to do with that earlier conception of a "more fully human life". That notion, it turns out, is central to any effort we make to help other people. Indeed, it determines both the kind and the range of any help we try to give. And helping other people, as you recall, was central to leading a moral life.

CHAPTER 10

<u>Helping Other People and</u> <u>"Spiritual Awakening"</u>

How one conceives of that "more fully human life" we've been talking about will determine how you try to help other people. And the critical difference, it turns out, comes in the area of "the spiritual" as we have been discussing it. If you believe as the SH does, then "helping others" would involve one set of activities. If you believe as the RS does, then "helping others' would involve that same set of activities <u>plus</u> another set. And that other set may actually be seen by the RS as ultimately even more important than the first set.

For the SH, "helping other people" would primarily involve what could be summarized by referring to the beatitudes. Or, as we described them earlier, helping people in the areas of food, shelter, clothing, health care and education. The basics that are virtually universally acknowledged to be needed in order to live a moderately comfortable and humane life, to pursue one's goals and to be content.

The RS would agree (after all the Beatitudes were originally given in a religious context), but they would add that there is another dimension that it is good for people to know about and to incorporate into their lives. A dimension that involves those two additional beliefs (and assumptions) that we discussed in Ch. 8, the assumptions concerning meaning and value. If those beliefs are true, and the RS certainly believes that they are true, then coming to be aware of that truth and incorporating it into one's life plays an important role in realizing a "more fully human" life.

For the Buddhist, coming to this awareness is referred to as "spiritual awakening", and it is the result of a rather long (commonly) and rigorous meditation practice. (Though to even begin such a meditation practice presumes at least a provisional acceptance of the spiritual realm as the RS conceives of it. This provisional acceptance is reflected in the first two steps of the Buddha's eightfold path.)

> On the other hand, there is a currently quite popular kind of Buddhist-like meditation practice where such a provisional acceptance of the RS's view is not required. I'm referring to the mindfulness based stress reduction kind of meditation practice. (Hereafter, MBSR.) In this practice, the purpose of the meditation is not necessarily to achieve awakening or enlightenment in the classic spiritual sense, but rather to learn how to moderate and control one's emotional and even physical responses to the various stresses and strains in life, whether surprising and unplanned or expected and foreseen. I say "not necessarily" because some of the practitioners of MBSR may very well be pursuing it as part of a classic Buddhist meditation practice. But there are clearly many who practice it with absolutely no commitment to the spiritual underpinnings as understood by a traditional Buddhist.

The classic Buddhist meditation practice is thought to lead, eventually and hopefully, to enlightenment, a coming to see the way 'things' *really* are. Never having experienced enlightenment, I cannot say what it is like. But there are enough commentaries from people who have (claimed to have) experienced it, that we can give an approximation of what is 'seen' in such an experience.

And the essence of such a "spiritual awakening" is that 'things' are very different from what they appear to be from an obvious or cursory or unexamined view. It results in the conviction that "something else is going on." A shorthand description for this way that 'things' seem to be is "illusory," and 'seeing' that illusoriness is to overcome ignorance that is thought of as one of the main hindrances to both happiness and nirvana.

Such illusoriness is not new nor is it peculiar to Buddhist thought. Here, e.g., is a description from Alan Lightman's review of the book <u>Light</u> by Bruce Watson of such illusoriness at the level of our simple, everyday interactions in the world.

> "If the book has a climax, it is in one of the final chapters, titled "Einstein and the Quanta, Particle, and Wave," where Watson celebrates the ultimate enigma of light — that it acts both like waves, simultaneously spread over an extended region of space, and particles, each located at only one point of space at a time. Such seemingly mutually exclusive descriptions *violate our human experience with the world*. That enigma reaches far beyond light. It applies to all of reality at the tiny scale of the atom. Above all else, *modern physics has shown us that what we humans perceive with our limited bodies, and all of our notions based on those perceptions, **are an illusion**,* an approximation of a strange cosmos we can touch only with our instruments and equations."   [Emph. mine]

An even simpler (but seldom reflected upon) example of the illusoriness I'm speaking of here – at this very basic level of our sensory perceptions – is the realization that the rose is not red. There is no color red that is in the rose.

This level of illusoriness is at the physical level. It is perceived and acknowledged by the most rigorous empirical scientist. But there are other levels as well and here is where it gets more difficult to see. For example, at the levels of our conceptual structuring and understanding of the world we inhabit, and at the most personal level of all, at the level of what we think our 'self' is or isn't.

In the first of these "other levels" of illusoriness, an example would be coming to realize that our structuring of the universe in a subject-object kind of way is just that, a way we structure the universe and our experience of it. It is not necessarily the way the universe is, and according to the enlightenment experience is, in fact, not the way the universe actually is.

And at the next "other level", it's coming to realize that the self we usually picture to ourselves, that self-same, persisting through time, substantial entity which we've labeled our self, does not actually exist *in that way*. It is not a substance with its own inherent existence but is more like a stream of consciousness that has some continuity to it but is also constantly changing. At its apex, the enlightenment at this level is sometimes described as the disappearance of the self or the experience of no-self. Alternatively, I have seen it described as an experience in which the thinker, the thought and the thing thought about all merge into one.

As I've said, I have not experienced this. I'm simply reporting here some of the descriptions that others have given of their experience. Nevertheless, I think we can easily imagine how having such an experience might profoundly affect how a person lives and how they interact in the world subsequent to such an experience.

> And here also there is room for interpretation. In a recent book, for example, (*Waking Up*), Sam Harris describes very similar reports of experiences that he has had in his own meditation practice, but he stops decidedly short of thinking that such experiences indicate anything transcendent. They do, he thinks, indicate a way in which we can "transcend" the self. But that seems to mean only that if the experience is veridical, then the way we normally conceive of our self is a mistake, and we thus *transcend* that mistaken view and arrive at a more accurate view of the self. But not one that involves any sense of transcendence in the religious sense we have been looking at.

As was mentioned before, what is paramount in such an experience is the conviction it results in, namely that "something else is going on." And that something else implies an unseen reality, something behind or underneath or extending far beyond the "illusory" reality that we are constantly interacting with in our evolutionary, survival mode. If you believe it, it stands to reason that it would have a significant affect on how one lives one's life.

This ending belief is similar for the Abrahamic religions though they get to it in quite different ways (usually <u>not</u> experientially) and interpret that "unseen reality" in different ways as well. But what is the same is that such a view of things changes everything. The Beatitudes, though important, are not the end of the story. There is also this new perspective which changes what is seen as really important, what is really valuable and worth seeking and, in our current context, what's fully involved in "helping other people."

For the RS, then, helping other people achieve a "more fully human life" goes beyond the beatitude-like activities we outlined above. It also includes this "spiritual awakening" we have been speaking of. But, of course, it can't be forced on anyone. It can be spoken of, offered as a goal, encouraged, but ultimately it's up to the individual to accept it or not, to try to realize it or not.

> And in this, I think it must be said, the Buddhists have generally been much better than the Abrahamic religions at acknowledging and respecting that such a belief, such an insight, cannot be forced on anyone. It's something each must come to on their own accord. A decision to pursue such a vision that each must make for him or herself.

CHAPTER 11

<u>Choosing Between Competing Worldviews</u>

The first thing to note is that either worldview is possible; i.e. those assumptions and axioms do describe possible states-of-affairs. Either *could* be the case. Neither contains within itself any outright irrationalities or contradictions. Each system or worldview is consistent within itself. (Compare e.g., to Euclidean geometry and non-Euclidean geometries that we referenced before.)

And because these assumptions which define, support and structure each respective worldview, those of the SH and of the RS, are consistent and comprehensive, they constitute a theory, an explanatory framework. But each theory is actually prior to the experiences they are used to define, interpret and understand.

Not prior in a strictly historical sense, of course. A baby's initial interactions with the wider world are a pretty unstructured mishmash of incoming data. But amazingly quickly, the baby learns and is taught how to interpret such data. And from then on, most subsequent incoming data is interpreted and understood in accordance with the explanatory theory they've been provided. (And of course, it is not seen or thought of as an "explanatory *theory*" either by the baby or its parents.)

But such frameworks <u>are prior in an analytical sense,</u> they provide the categories and the connections by which any incoming data is sorted and interrelated. They are <u>methodologically prior</u>. And this is exactly why Einstein could make that statement referenced earlier to Werner Heisenberg: 'Remember Werner, what we see is determined by the theory we use to interpret our observations.' And if we substitute in the word 'experience' for the words 'see' and 'observations' in the above statement, the claim remains the same. The theory or the worldview we use to interpret our experience is somehow both prior to and interdependent upon that experience itself.

Thus, whether we adopt the SH worldview or that of the RS, either one will determine how we interpret the raw, incoming data of our experience. And though each worldview shares a great deal so that much of our experience is understood and interpreted the same under either framework or theory or worldview, there are times when the worldviews diverge dramatically and at those times, any experience we might have is understood and interpreted in vastly different, often diametrically opposed, ways.

And, it appears, there is no strictly discursive way of deciding between such worldviews. Within themselves, they are logically consistent. And in their common elements, they can and often do agree in their interpretations and explanations. So then, what is one to do? Is there no alternative but arbitrary choice?

There may be an alternative, namely a non-discursive way of deciding between them, a way that constitutes an almost aesthetic-like judgment.

And like an aesthetic judgment, **the first** step in such a process is at a very unarticulated, gut level. It simply asks: which of the competing worldviews *feels* the most compatible to you, all things considered? The answer to this question alone doesn't settle anything. It just references a feeling state which is important to recognize and honor, but is not decisive.

For example, the SH would say that the variety and complexity of the animal kingdom is the result of a non-intentional, purely mechanical, sorting system working over an incredibly long time-period. Whereas the RS would say that though the SH may have accurately described the mechanics, the *how*, of the development of the animal kingdom, these mechanics themselves did not appear just by chance but that they are the result of intelligence and intention. Which *seems* the most plausible to you?

Similarly, the SH might say that the moral rules which mankind has developed to help govern the interactions between people are, as a matter of fact, simply the result of successive iterations of attempts to come up with rules that most people in any given social group deem fair and are willing to live by. And that these rules do not reflect or reveal any underlying reality or any absolute sense in which right and wrong or good and evil exist.

Whereas the RS might say that such rules or, at least, many of them, actually do capture something inherent in the notions of right and wrong, and of good and evil, something which is independent of any simple pragmatic agreement among individuals whether real or imagined. And again, which *seems* the most plausible to you? Which *feels* the best to you?

Now, as I've said, this feeling state is certainly not determinative of which worldview is the more correct. On the other hand, it may well be indicative of a resonance within the person that should not be ignored. As Pascal has said: "the heart has its reasons about which the mind knows nothing."

The second consideration to help one decide which worldview to adopt is to ask: which worldview (or explanatory framework or theory) explains (or finds a place for) <u>the most of what we experience?</u> And the "we" in this sentence refers both to you as an individual and to all other humans throughout recorded history. (Subject, of course, to our own limitations in knowing about such experiences.)

All other things being equal, if one theory explains, finds a place for, <u>more</u> of the data to be explained, that theory should

112

be the one adopted, at least provisionally. [The "all other things being equal" clause refers to the fact that both of the theories under consideration, that of the SH and that of the RS, are here, and after the discussion above, taken to be internally consistent and with no obvious contradictions or irrationalities.]

And the tipping point here would seem to be in the area of so-called mystical experience. For the RS, the explanation is that the subject is experiencing something transcendent by means of or through their own consciousness, albeit something which cannot be empirically demonstrated or proven based on incontestable premises, and something that is not adequately captured in concepts and categories nor adequately expressed in language. All such attempts must therefore be, at least in part, metaphorical.

For the SH, such experiences are ranked, broadly, in the category of hallucinations or delusions. They do not reveal anything existent outside of or independent of the individual's mind.

So in this case, both worldviews <u>have</u> found a place for such experiences, they do have a way of explaining them, just very different ways indeed. So it doesn't seem that the second consideration for selecting between worldviews would be determinative here. Both of the worldviews under consideration <u>have</u> found a place for; have an explanation for, all aspects of our own and of the broader range of human experiences.

In which case, we might then refer back to that first criterion and ask: which of these two explanations of so-called mystical experience *seems* the most plausible?

The final consideration I want to suggest for use in deciding between worldviews is: which worldview ends up being the more life-affirming, the more helpful in getting through life, the more hopeful?

This also relates to our earlier discussion on wishful thinking. At one level, the level of purely rational analysis, using this as a criterion for deciding between worldviews can be seen as simply more begging of the question. It *assumes* that the more life-affirming, the more helpful, worldview is or is likely to be the more correct one. But if the SH's worldview is right about things, then such a criterion is itself merely wishful thinking and not at all an indication that the worldview is correct.

But on another level, on a level more inclusive than that of the purely rational, the level that includes the desire for that fuller human existence we've talked about from the beginning, the level that focuses on the kind of person you want to be and the kind of life you want to live, on that level this consideration may be telling.

Judging based on numbers alone, the RS's have it . . . .

But, of course, numbers alone are no guarantee of truth.

And maybe that's the point. There is no guarantee of truth in adopting one or the other of these worldviews. Here, the purely intellectual approach just can't settle the issue. Which worldview most helps you become the person you want to be and to live the life you want to live (and to have lived)?

For this to be used as a general criterion, of course, one must assume that virtually everyone would want to live and to achieve that "more fully human" existence that we have been talking about. And that such a "more fully human life" is not something that can be filled in in just any, arbitrary, fashion but that certain sorts of activities and goals, behaviors and efforts and habits are to be preferred and sought after, are actually good for us as humans. And that living in this way will lead to the most peace, satisfaction and 'happiness' achievable, both for the individual and for all individuals.

Which of these worldviews most helps *you* to live the life *you* want to live? Which leads to the most 'happiness' for you?

PART IV

SUMMARY AND CONCLUSIONS

CHAPTER 12

The Final Picture

You've got some time now (in your retirement years). How are you going to spend it?

Under either understanding of the 'spiritual' that we've been examining–the secular humanist interpretation or the religious interpretation– it appears that pursuing the 'spiritual' in one's life can be seen as the "highest and best" activity that we can engage in. That activity which expresses and fulfills those most noble parts of our natures and personalities. Aesthetic appreciation; intellectual curiosity, investigation and coming to know what is so; treating others with dignity and respect, kindness and consideration. All of these combine to help us live the "most fully human life" we can live.

And doing this latter (striving for the "most fully human life" we can) would seem to be an unalloyed and self-evident good. Indeed, it is constantly used, sometimes explicitly, at other times implicitly, in both our private and public discussions to justify positions we take and want to promote on everything from educational and social policy to raising our children. (Ch.'s 1&2)

In addition, the religious 'spiritual' claims that there is a whole other dimension to our existence that does not conflict with or contradict this "more fully human life", but which puts it into an expanded context. It's almost like going from a two dimensional view of things to a three dimensional one.

What a great opportunity!

Enjoy the beautiful, search for the truth and do some good. Freed at last from the daily concerns of making a living and raising a family, you can finally and fully focus on the question which has periodically and persistently troubled many (all?) of us over the years: "What's it all about Alfie?" Or, perhaps more clearly: is this all there is?

And this search for what it's all about led us, in this book, to consider the 'spiritual' – led us to consider whether there was "anything more" to our lives than simply the here-and-now, the cares and concerns, the trials and tribulations, the successes and failures, the "good, the bad and the ugly" that characterize our lives from birth to death. It has led us to consider whether "something else" is going on. And as we searched for the truth about the 'spiritual' we discovered that

One can't escape from either Metaphysics or Epistemology. (In the form of basic, axiomatic-like, beliefs held by each side in this debate).

When we looked at each of the major positions on the 'spiritual', we discovered that in each case they depended on certain basic beliefs or assumptions that were taken by their respective adherents as essentially being beyond argument or not needing argument. They were the givens on which both the SH (the secular humanist, here taken as equivalent to the materialist or the naturalist) and the RS (the religious spiritualist) built their respective worldviews. Sometimes these assumptions were metaphysical in nature (dealing with what exists and what can exist), and sometimes they were epistemological in nature (dealing with what we can know and how). But in both cases, it turned out that you simply couldn't hold the position without believing in one or the other set of these assumptions or, at least, in the main assumption of each set. (See Ch's 4&5)

In addition, one can't escape from certain assumptions in the realms of meaning and value. (Ch. 8)

Assumptions about whether there is "any point to it all" and whether character <u>is</u> destiny (whether the universe is lawful in the moral realm as it is in the physical). We likened these to components in the RS's TOE or theory of everything. And together, these basic assumptions in the realms of metaphysics and epistemology as well as meaning and value, comprised the final worldviews of each, the SH and the RS.

And we then wondered, so where does that leave us? Trapped in an irresolvable dilemma? "There is nothing beyond the physical and whatever is caused by the physical" or "no, something does exist which is neither physical nor dependent upon the physical for its existence." And between "the universe <u>is</u> lawful in the moral realm" and "no, the universe <u>is not</u> lawful in the moral realm." And we concluded, perhaps not. Perhaps we are not trapped in an irresolvable dilemma. Rather, we can

Then use these basic sets of assumptions or axioms to help you decide which position, which worldview, <u>you</u> find most compatible.

There is no avoiding it. Each of us must decide, whether consciously or by default, what we believe in this regard. And in Ch. 11 I suggested that we might well be guided in making such a decision by asking: which worldview most helps *me* live the life I want to live and to be happy? But in this approach, there was the assumption that "the life I want to live" involves that more fully human existence we have been talking about all along, and a 'happiness' that is a genuine happiness (as opposed to an hedonic happiness).

And in this, no one can answer for another person. There is no logical argument, so far as I can see, that would condemn either side in this debate, the SH or the RS, to a rank inconsistency if they hold either worldview and still choose to be kind and considerate toward all others.

'Happiness' however may be another matter. For me, I must confess, it is hard to imagine a nihilistic stance (the position that neither existence nor values have any lasting meaning) being compatible with happiness, as we have been interpreting that notion. (But then, to the nihilist, I suppose, 'happiness' is not a value, not a state worth desiring.)

And it was suggested that this concordance, this compatibility, between one or other of these worldviews and your own desires for and practice of a life well-lived may well be, in the end, the best criterion to use in deciding which worldview to adopt.

There is no one answer for everyone. For some, the SH's position may fill this role. While seeming depressing and wholly negative to others, to some it may seem simply realistic, the most obvious and mature, the one least prone to wishful and ultimately misleading thinking. While for others, the RS's position seems the most plausible; perhaps because of the range of human experience it finds a place for in its schema or the place it finds for such experiences. Or maybe because the ultimate trust and hope it supports resonates with their own deepest desires and intuitions.

And if that is so, why not rest in an appeal to these other aspects of our being to help us decide? If either worldview can be seen as equally rational, i.e. as following from and consistent with a given set of assumptions– (such as those above), then why not go with something beyond the purely rational to help one decide? And if that, why not go with whatever helps you achieve or realize the best you you can conceive of? Referring back to Pascal again:

"The heart has its reasons, about which the mind knows nothing."

And in the Buddhist tradition, there is this:

"Quiet the mind and open the heart."

Is there no difference then? Am I saying that there is no practical and significant difference which results from adopting either the SH's meaning of 'spiritual' or the RS's meaning? That which is true makes no difference here and now? At least, not *necessarily* any difference?

No, no. It does make a difference. But not in the realm of "chopping wood and carrying water," not in the work-a-day world of survival and practical living. Rather, it makes a difference in the area of that "more fully human life" and what counts as such. And it does so through that notion of "spiritual awakening". For the RS, that involves seeing one's life in a wholly different context and the consequences of one's actions extending beyond one's current earthly existence. Not so for the SH. And for the RS, one has not realized a "more fully human life" unless and until one realizes the "illusory" nature of this life. And, again, for the SH, not so.

> In Zen Buddhism there is the story of a young aspirant who imagines marvelous and great wonders following upon enlightenment, and asks his master about the effects of enlightenment on one's life. The master responds that before enlightenment, one must "chop wood and carry water." I.e., one must attend to the nitty gritty, normal, daily activities involved in staying alive and living as a monk. But, after enlightenment, ... one must still "chop wood and carry water." The requirements for staying alive and living as a monk have not changed. One does not become an ethereal being floating through life and existing on air. Any enlightenment does not change the basic needs for living.

So, the difference it makes, then, <u>is in the worldview</u> one holds? Well, that and in any consequences that follow for one from holding and acting in accord with that worldview.

And given that, from a purely rational standpoint, one cannot determine which worldview is correct, it seems reasonable to use those consequences to help one decide which worldview to hold.

And thus we have our "spiritual guide for retirement" spoken of in the book's title.

Namely, seek out this very personal truth; discern between and adopt whichever of these worldviews <u>most helps you</u> help others, whichever most helps you practice kindness and compassion for all . . . . and then, of course, actually practice them.

Postscript:

For those who adopt the RS's worldview, there is a classical metaphysical framework within which to place that worldview. It is basically **a levels analysis**. The relatively real and the absolutely real. The 'real' that we interact with and negotiate through in our daily human existence. The world of water and trees, other bodies and personalities, a world of health and survival. A world that is constantly in flux, constantly changing. In the famous Zen phrase: the world of "chopping wood and carrying water". And then there is the 'real' that does not change, that has always been and will not cease to be. As the Buddha had it in Udana 8.3

> "*There is* a not-born, not-made, not-brought into being, not-conditioned . . ."

> [Emph. mine]

And this levels analysis has a long tradition. Classically, there is the level of the relatively real, the world of our sense experience e.g. Plato's shadows on the wall of the cave, and the level of the absolutely real, that from which all else comes and on which all else depends. In Plato's allegory, the sun outside the cave played this role. (And in some traditions, there are also intermediate levels of reality, in Plato, the forms, in Christianity, the level of angels and demons, in Buddhism, the level of the devas, and in Islam, the jinn, e.g.)

Such a levels analysis allows and respects the reality of the physical universe, but it also affirms and honors the reality of a transcendent.

INDEX

Printed in the United States
By Bookmasters